Travels with John and Gwen

A Combat Medic and His Wife
Explore the World after WWII

Travels with John and Gwen

A Combat Medic and His Wife
Explore the World after WWII

JOHN A. KERNER, MD

iBooks
New York

iBooks
Manhanset House
Dering Harbor, New York 11965-0342
bricktower@aol.com
www.BrickTowerPress.com

All rights reserved under the International and Pan-American Copyright Conventions. No part of this publication may be reproduced, stored in a retrieval system, or transmitted in any form or by any means, electronic or otherwise, without the prior written permission of the copyright holder.

The iBooks colophon is a trademark
of J. Boylston & Company, Publishers.

Library of Congress Cataloging-in-Publication Data
Travels with John and Gwen: A Combat Medic and His Wife
Explore the World after WWII
Kerner, MD, John A.

p. cm.
TRAVEL / Essays & Travelogues
BIOGRAPHY & AUTOBIOGRAPHY / Personal Memoirs
Copyright © 2022 by John A. Kerner, MD
ISBN: 978-1-59687-029-1
Editor: Rose Marie Cleese
Interior Design/Typeset: Mike Slizewski
Cover Design: David Newman
First Printing 2022

This book is lovingly dedicated
to the memory of
Gwendolyn Miller Kerner.

TABLE OF CONTENTS

About This Book — *i*

Preface — *iii*

Acknowledgments — *xiii*

Chapter One: London • 1958 – *1*

Chapter Two: Paris • 1958 / French Riviera • 1964 — *15*

Chapter Three: Venice • 1958 — *25*

Chapter Four: Florence • 1958 — *35*

Chapter Five: Rome • 1958 / Lake Como • 1991 — *45*

Chapter Six: Ireland • 1993 — *51*

Chapter Seven: Berlin • 2001 — *57*

Chapter Eight: Africa: Kenya, Zimbabwe, and Botswana • 1977 / Egypt • 1980 — *66*

Chapter Nine: Southeast Asia: Burma (Myanmar) • 1983 / Cambodia • 1996 — *80*

Chapter Ten: Japan • 1975 and 1992 — *85*

Chapter Eleven: China • 1981 — *94*

Chapter Twelve: South America • 1994 — *107*

Chapter Thirteen: New York City • 1958–2016 — *115*

Chapter Fourteen: Return to the WWII Battlefields • 2003 — *126*

Chapter Fifteen: Washington, DC—French Legion of Honor Medal • 2007 — *138*

About the Author — *149*

ABOUT THIS BOOK

A little more than a decade after the end of the Second World War, although my medical practice in San Francisco was in its early years and we didn't have much money, my wife, Gwen, and I had a lot of friends who had been to Europe, and it whetted our appetite to do likewise. In addition, I was anxious to show Gwen some of the places I had passed through when I was a combat medic during World War II.

We enjoyed our first trip together (to Europe in 1958) so much that, from then on, we took a trip somewhere once or twice a year, sometimes more. During those sublime, peaceful times a decade after WWII and after the conclusions of the Korean and Vietnam wars, Gwen and I traveled extensively. In those six decades since that first European trip, we went on nearly ninety foreign trips that ranged from visits to cosmopolitan world capitals to forays into wilderness areas. This was in addition to countless trips we made to every corner of the United States. One of the most wonderful things about our travels is that they allowed Gwen and me to spend time together in fascinating environments surrounded by captivating personalities. We talked to everyone, from everyday residents to royalty, and Gwen was always able to rise to the occasion and converse with anyone.

Another thing that our travels gifted us with was that all those many exciting and special occasions we experienced enhanced our personal relationship, both physically and mentally, over the years. I think this was one of the main motivations for our traveling so much. We left behind our kids (well cared for), my patients, the housework, etc. We were "far from the madding crowd's ignoble strife," to quote the English poet Thomas Gray. I'm fairly certain our many travels are why we were so in love with each other right up to the day Gwen passed away in 2021, very close to our seventy-fifth wedding anniversary.

Our travel adventures came to a crashing end before Gwen's death, however, with the advent of the COVID-19 virus. But that unfortunate cessation of travel gave me the time to reflect on some of the experiences we had during all those harmonious years. I am concerned that we may never live in that world again. It was such a unique time in our history, when people could travel unhindered and worry-free to so many corners of the world. It is my hope that my sharing some of our adventures and insights with you in this book will give you a taste of the world Gwen and I were fortunate enough to wander about in.

Gwen and John Kerner

PREFACE

My international travels all started upon my arrival as a combat medic to join the 35th Infantry Division in England, where we were to prepare for the invasion of Europe in World War II. I had never been outside the United States as an adult, with the exception of a transit of the Panama Canal when moving from the West Coast to the East Coast as a child. Though I knew our purpose for being in England, I was hoping to see some of the country, having read so much English literature in my lifetime. We landed in Liverpool on May 25, 1944, after a long voyage from New York—long because we had zigzagged a lot, trying to avoid submarine attacks. We landed at night. The city was being bombed repeatedly, and there were numerous fires. There was a blackout, of course, yet there were British soldiers waiting to direct us, and girls giving out doughnuts. We were not allowed to dally, however. We were put on waiting trains as night turned to day, and I didn't get to see much of Liverpool. We enjoyed seeing the girls, though.

As we moved away from Liverpool, the countryside spread out on a clear warm day. We opened the windows on the train and were overwhelmed by the beauty of the landscape. We rarely saw such lush green in California. Well-tended hedges whose patterns extended as far as the eye could see divided the fields in that part of the country. Fat cattle populated the fields. Every so often we came upon a home or cluster of homes, all constructed of bright red, rough bricks, with gray slate or red tile roofs. Every home had a garden with trees, and the villages we saw were neat and clean.

Our destination was the town of Bodmin, where we were to train for the coming invasion. It was wonderful. The railroad station was surrounded by rhododendron bushes. As soon as I got a chance, I wandered down to town. Visiting the shops was a particular joy. I loved using their currency and had quite a bit of it, having won various card games on the sea voyage over. Prices were low. For instance, I bought Sadler's Boot Polish for 8d (about 13 cents). Bodmin was built mainly along one street. There were shops, the hotel where I was put with a bunch of low-level officers, and a number of lovely, well-maintained homes. And there was a church that had been badly damaged in the recent "blitz." What this tiny, charming town did for me was to increase my desire to see more.

Whenever my unit needed supplies, I volunteered to go with a driver. So, I was able to visit Plymouth and Exeter. I made friends with a girl in Plymouth and a woman in Bodmin that added to my visits. This enthusiasm for seeing new places would turn out to dilute the hard times I would be facing during our battles in France and beyond in the coming months.

My wartime experience took me to Omaha Beach, Saint-Lô, Mortain, Le Mans, Nancy, Metz, Bastogne, Maastricht, Hanover, Brussels, Paris twice, and many more locales. At the end of my European duty, London was my last stop before heading back home to the US. So, when I married Gwen, I could hardly wait to take her to see these places—and the rest of the world.

***

My travels, I must add, began well before my wartime introduction to Europe, thanks to my father, Simon Kapstein, who was employed by the F.W. Woolworth Company. As a boy he worked in minor jobs with E.P. Charlton and Company before joining Woolworth's. In his early twenties, he began opening Woolworth stores in the western United States and Canada (his grandmother wouldn't let him travel for work until he was twenty-one years old). He continued that job until he opened and managed a store in Portland, Oregon, where I was born in 1919. Although I started my life in Portland, the family moved to San Francisco shortly thereafter, when my father relocated to the Woolworth store at the corner of Powell and Market Streets in the heart of the city. As the Woolworth Company paid managers a percentage of their net profits, after a few years he was earning more than anyone in the Woolworth Company except the president. Although he had friends in the company, there was much jealousy among employees because of his position. In addition, there was a good deal of anti-Semitism within the Woolworth Company. . .and in the country as well.

When I was in seventh grade, my father retired at an early age, having enough savings and investments, and my family moved from San Francisco to Chestnut Hill, a suburb of Boston. My father thought it would be good to live close to Boston to be near the rest of his family. We had many relatives in the area. When we moved to Boston, we went by ship, the SS *Virginia*, through the Panama Canal, with a major stop in Havana, Cuba. We had once traveled across the country to visit my maternal grandmother and grandfather in Fall River, Massachusetts, but this was my first time outside of the United States. Accompanying us on the voyage was our seven-passenger Cadillac and our cook. When we arrived in Boston, we got settled into our new home. My father had bought a beautiful house there on a large lot of land in an elegant suburb. And I acquired a wirehaired fox terrier. I went to school in Boston at the Boston Latin School, which required high grades at one's previous school for entrance. This school changed my life, because I got all As, an accomplishment that followed me through high school and medical school.

My mother, Jeanette, who loved New York City, took me there often. Her favorite cousin in New York was a buyer for Saks Fifth Avenue, and she was always giving us theater tickets to Broadway shows, such as the radically new type of musical called *Oklahoma*. This generosity of my mother's cousin instilled in me a lifelong love of the theater. My father also took me to New York City to show me the major highlights. We visited the city's iconic landmarks, the Metropolitan Museum of Art, and his favorite restaurants.

Then came the financial crash of 1929. Luckily, my father had sold all his stocks when their value was high, but the rest of the family was hurt by the crash, and he bailed them all out. At that point, he decided to return to the San Francisco Bay Area, where he felt more at home in trying to create a new fortune.

So, we moved back to San Francisco, where my father built a beautiful home in Sea Cliff. I first went to a public school in Pacific Heights before attending Galileo High School. From there, I followed my sister, Dorothy, to college at the University of California at Berkeley, where I enrolled in the premed program. (I had a taste of the university before I went there, having used my sister's student body card to attend football games.)

While I was at Galileo High School, war was looming, and all the male students had to join ROTC, where I became a captain. In college, we had to take Navy ROTC because UC Berkeley was a land grant university. While in the premed program, I lived in a boarding house where one of my roommates was a chap named Eldred Peck who was enrolled in the drama department and later, substituting his first name with his middle name, was known as the acclaimed movie actor, Gregory Peck! My main memory of him was of his being on a championship rowing crew. He was so exhausted from rowing that he was often plastered on his bed.

I had a professor of history at Berkeley who was a great teacher, and he predicted that we would be at war with Japan and most likely Germany. After the Japanese bombed Pearl Harbor in 1941, the Japanese medical students we attended class with were removed from the premed program. At least two of them had been friends of mine since grammar school. I complained bitterly to the authorities. At one point, my professor called me in and said that if I kept complaining about the Japanese medical students being taken out of school, even though they had been born here and were US citizens, the school might kick me out. He said this was an official government order. Thankfully, some of the Japanese students got admitted into medical schools in the Midwest, but still it was a sad time for our country.

From Berkeley, I went on to UC's medical school in San Francisco where I did pretty well and was elected to Phi Beta Kappa and the Alpha Omega Alpha Honor Medical Society. (It was possible to qualify for medical school in three years if one took the right courses and had good grades.) Before the US actually entered the war, we had to choose which branch of service we would join, and I chose the Army. Halfway through my medical internship at UCSF, where I was serving as an OB-GYN intern, I got notice that I had been drafted into the Army while I was scrubbing for surgery with my professor. The Army gave me four days to report for duty. I got the orders on a Friday and was told to report for duty in Pennsylvania on the following Tuesday.

A friend of mine, who was already serving as a pilot in Burma, happened to be on leave and helped me get together the things I needed before enlisting. He took me to see a friend of his who was a CEO, Sam Zeigler, and he helped me get equipped with combat clothes at the Presidio. Hastings Clothing Company, a men's store in downtown San Francisco, was able to fit me with a dress uniform in one day, a uniform I ended up hardly ever wearing, because we usually wore our combat uniforms once deployed. When I returned from overseas, my dress uniform was in such pristine condition, I kept it and actually wore it when receiving the French Legion of Honor award in Washington, DC, in 2007. Thanks to Sammy Zeigler, I was one of very few who had a winter military uniform when I arrived in Pennsylvania to be assigned. I was grateful to have warm clothes when we went out into the cold for our drills.

My first assignment was at Wakeman General Hospital in Denver, Colorado, which was heaven. Even though I had gotten only halfway through my internship at UCSF, I was assigned to do surgery on my first day. One of my first patients was a pilot, and since he was confined to the hospital, he let me use his car and gas coupons. I really was so happy in that situation, being able to get around. After finishing my internship, I was then assigned to the 10th Mountain Division in Colorado. I was with that division only a short time, however, as I was then reassigned to join an infantry division that, unbeknownst to any of us at the time, was scheduled to take part in the invasion of France at Normandy.

Before I went off to Europe, I started gathering supplies for my tour. Cotton gauze strips were standard issue in the military ever since World War I, but I thought elastic bandages (aka Ace bandages), which were a fairly new thing in the medical community, would be much better when in combat. I wasn't sure I'd be able to find them in Europe, so I gathered up as many as I could while still in the US.

While I was stationed in Bodmin, England, I continued looking for medical supplies and took different routes on each supply run to see as much of southwest England as I could. A short time before the invasion, we were moved to a secret base and were reviewed by Generals Dwight D. Eisenhower and George S. Patton. Churchill also came to review our unit, because we were part of the spearhead of the invasion. We were put on landing crafts on the 5th of June, but they decided to postpone the invasion, dubbed Operation Overlord. Our men were so seasick the next day that we were unable to join the first launch of the invasion (D-Day), which probably saved our lives. A few days later, with me serving as a combat medic, our unit, the 110th Medical Battalion, landed on Omaha Beach. Our unit was a collection company; our role was to collect the wounded from the battlefields. Shortly after we landed, we were escorted off the beach as quickly as possible by the MPs. The Germans knew our weaknesses. During the initial days of the invasion, two of the doctors in the 35th Division were killed at a battalion station, and given the division's large number of wounded, I was reassigned to that division. As far as I have been able to determine, I believe I was the first doctor to be awarded a medal during those first days of Operation Overlord. I stayed with my collection unit throughout my European tour and gained the respect of my men.

When the war ended in Europe, my unit was told that we would be sent home before being deployed to take part in the invasion of Japan. First, we would be sailing by ship from Southampton to the US, but we would have some free time in England before we embarked. We sailed on the *Queen Mary*, which was an incredible contrast to the war conditions we had been living under. The ship was beautiful and the food amazing. We landed in New Jersey and were given priority for plane flights due to the fact that we were scheduled to go to Japan soon. The military personnel told me that if I was willing to fly home using some of my many service points, I could be booked on a flight to San Francisco immediately. I took them up on it and traveled west across the country on what was my very first plane flight, surprising my parents with my early arrival.

Shortly after I arrived back in San Francisco, I thought I would look up some of my old girlfriends. My favorite girlfriend was away at school at the University of Oregon, and I found most of the other old girlfriends uninteresting after having been away at war.

My mother and one of her friends were upset that I wasn't interested in any of these women. I wasn't in a great place and concentrated instead on making a notebook about my time in the war. This scrapbook is now in an alumni memorabilia museum at UC Berkeley. At one point, my "yenta" duo insisted that I go out on this blind date. So, I gave in, asked the young woman in question out on a date, and picked her up at her parents' home in St. Francis Wood. Her name was Gwen Miller, and I found her to be the most beautiful woman and a splendid dancer. She had graduated from Stanford with a Phi Beta Kappa award and was very intelligent.

Even though the dropping of the atomic bombs in Japan put an end to the military's planned deployments across the Pacific, the Army was still not ready to release me from duty. So I was sent to a hospital in Indianapolis, Indiana, where the head doctor there said, "What would you like to do in this hospital?" He mentioned that plastic surgery was the best department at that hospital, so, I asked to be assigned there. The stitching skill I acquired while there proved to be very useful during my career when delivering babies.

While I was in Indianapolis, I got a letter every day from Gwen—letters that I still have. I was surprised that she was interested in me, but pleased and flattered. I thought she was the perfect partner. We agreed to get married after I figured out that I could afford to support us. My residency wasn't paying very much, but then the GI Bill paid me supplemental money for more education and toward my residency salary. I had been worried that I wouldn't be earning enough to tie the knot, but now it appeared that we could.

When I got back to San Francisco from Indianapolis, we got engaged while I was still considered active duty in the military. Around the time that I got drafted and had to depart for my military service in the Army, my mother had given me a ring that she had gotten made out of iron in San Francisco, which had her engagement diamond in a very simple but elegant setting. I wore it all through the war. Many women had tried to talk me out of that ring during my time overseas. I thought I should offer the ring to Gwen. When I decided that I was going to ask Gwen to marry me, I had the diamond taken out of its setting and took it to Laykin et Cie jewelers at I. Magnin & Co. I asked the jewelers there to design me an engagement ring, as I didn't like the style of the standard engagement rings that were in fashion then. They gave me two more-modern choices, and I choose the one made out of gold with four prongs holding the solitary diamond. When I went to pick up the ring, they billed me at a much higher price than the original quote they had given me. But when I protested, they said they would meet my budget for the ring, because they knew I would be a lifelong customer like the rest of my family. It turns out this ring design became a trendsetter, and they sold many more afterward. Once done with the war, I had accepted a position at San Francisco General Hospital. Gwen came to visit me at the hospital often before the wedding. She accepted the ring enthusiastically.

We got married on June 16, 1946, at the Mark Hopkins Hotel and spent our wedding night at the beautiful Fairmont Hotel, right across the street. We drove to Santa Barbara for our honeymoon. We couldn't go on a long trip because I was already working at SF General. The place I had wanted to stay in Santa Barbara was anti-Semitic, and because I had a Jewish last name, Kapstein, we decided not to stay there. (Our family had not yet changed our last name to Kerner.) A couple we knew told us about another hotel in Santa Barbara, and we stayed there. I never experienced any anti-Semitism in San Francisco, but I did experience it in the service and outside the Bay Area.

In the early years of our marriage, Gwen and I were busy raising a family—two sons and a daughter—and I was just starting out as a doctor. But I resolved that, as soon as we were able to, I would travel with Gwen, because there were so many places I had seen in the war that I wanted to show her. When the children were young, Gwen's mother was happy to stay with the children when we were away. Knowing that the children would be in good hands, we were able to start planning trips early in our marriage, and "travels with John and Gwen" began!

ACKNOWLEDGMENTS

This book would not have been possible without significant help from several friends, because I finished writing it when I was 102 years old. My beautiful wife, Gwen, passed away in April of 2021 after nearly seventy-five years of marriage. She was my best friend, an excellent travel partner—and the main motivating factor for writing this book. I think there may be a Volume Two in the future, if I live long enough.

Rose Marie Cleese, my amazing editor, has known me since she was my patient. Way back then, I told her about the book I was writing about my World War II experiences, *Combat Medic*, which was initially published in 2002. When the publisher of that book (my first) closed its doors, Rose Marie found me another publisher on the East Coast, and when it was up for a reprint, she did a full re-edit of the book (regrettably disallowed due to budget constraints). For this book, she helped me pare an enormous amount of material down to a reasonable length for a book. Her attention to detail is truly admirable. She has been so helpful with keeping me on track and has made my stories make sense. I really appreciate her excellent editing skills and our many years of friendship.

Manena Nichol Harper, my personal assistant for the last three years, laboriously typed up all my stories and memories and put them on paper. She collected and organized materials for the book from many sources. She catalogued photos from my more than twenty albums of photos for each chapter of the book. She stumbled upon a Japanese box filled with forty-plus years of Gwen's travel notes and took on the challenge of deciphering all of them, so that we could include many of the juicy bits that reflect Gwen's humor and personality. I really wanted Gwen's voice to be heard in this book, and I greatly appreciate Manena's dedication to this particular task and to the project in general.

David Newman, who also serves as my computer consultant, helped with the scanning of photos from the many volumes of photo albums from all of Gwen and my years of travel around the world. He spent many hours scanning them and enhancing them in a very professional way. He also created a book cover design, one of two for consideration. I really appreciate his dedication and willingness to work on this project, which I know was very challenging.

Publisher John Colby of iBooks and Brick Tower Press has been extremely supportive of me during the writing of this book, especially after my wife, Gwen, passed away last spring. He also published my last two books, as well as a reissue of my first book. He once shared with me that his father was also a World War II veteran, and I appreciate his willingness to allow me to share my stories with the world. I'm particularly grateful for the care and attention Mike Slizewski, John's editor and graphic designer/typesetter, took in formatting the book interior.

I extend a specially heartfelt thank you to Lute Naufahu 'Ahofono, my caregiver manager, for her excellent care and management of my team of caregivers over the last year. This excellent care has made it possible for me to live independently in my own home of the past twenty-five years in downtown San Francisco and has also enabled me to write and complete this book.

I want to thank my family—my sons John Kerner, Jr., MD, and James Kerner, and my daughter Jan Adrienne Harper—for their support of Gwen and me while the two of us embarked on our journeys, many of which occurred during their youth. Without their support all these years, our trips would never have happened. Ryan Kerner, my grandson, who designed the front book covers for my previous three books, also designed a cover candidate for this book, and I'm very grateful for his support and artistic contribution.

Last but not least, I want to thank my late wife, Gwen, wherever she may be, for all those minutes and hours and years and decades of truly blissful wandering. She added so much wit, light, love, and laughter to our adventures as we discovered so many corners of the world together, heart and soul and hand in hand.

John A. Kerner, MD
February 2022

P.S. All photos in this book were taken either by me, Gwen, a friend, or a helpful passerby, unless otherwise noted.

CHAPTER ONE

London • 1958

Gwen and I were married in June 1946, and I had gone into practice in 1949. It wasn't until 1958, when I was a resident in obstetrics and gynecology at UCSF, that we felt free to travel on the first of our eighty-nine trips. Gwen had given birth to two sons and and a daughter, and by now John, James, and Jan were old enough to be left in the care of Gwen's mother and a trusted maid. Previously, I had helped my parents plan a trip to Europe, and my sister and her husband had traveled to Europe as well. Although we didn't have a lot of money, we planned an ambitious trip to London, Paris, Venice, Florence, and Rome, with a stop in New York on the way home.

John and Gwen about to embark on one of their trips to Europe.

Our choice of airlines was Pan Am. Since this was before the jet age, our propeller-driven plane stopped in

New York en route to London in order to refuel. Much to our surprise, when we landed in New York, we were escorted off the plane to a pleasant restaurant atop New York International Airport (today's JFK International Airport), The Golden Door, where we could have anything we wanted for lunch. Gwen was impressed by the gold foil around the baked potatoes. By the time we'd finished lunch, the plane was ready to depart for London. We were traveling "tourist," the name for economy class back then. Can you imagine economy service like that nowadays?

> **From Gwen's travel diary**: *Flight from San Francisco to London, somewhere over the Atlantic Ocean—September 14, 1958. It is now 10:00 AM London time. I think we had four hours of sleep (the time changes every minute). Awakened! (My watch said 4:45 AM!). To a blinding clear day. Now, I feel we MIGHT make it. I'm getting excited. Very smooth night flight.*

Upon our arrival in London, at customs, we had to ask the officer to repeat each question at least once so we could understand his English. We were thrilled to be met by our friends, Jim and Laura Green, who were taking us to our hotel. What a lovely greeting that was. We had chosen a small hotel recommended by my secretary—The Green Park Inn on Half Moon Street in the lovely Mayfair district. The hotel was constructed by the joining of two large homes. When we got there we were exhausted, since we had slept only a few hours on our nine-hour, ten-minute flight from New York. The hotel was quite charming, with brightly painted doors framed by intricate wrought iron.

> **From Gwen's travel diary**: *Driven to [our hotel]—adorable and chic. So charming on the*

outside, funny and modern on the inside. [Our room has a] deep bathtub; the water faucets are reversed, with the cold on the left side.

The Green Park Inn, Mayfair District.

Although it was late morning, after unpacking a little and showering and bathing, we went to bed, falling asleep immediately. We were awakened by the sound of a man from the hotel staff entering our room who left when he saw we were resting. When we were through with our naps, we began to unpack. Gwen could not find the bag into which she had placed her valuables. We thought we had been robbed. We called the management, who promptly sent up a house officer. We looked everywhere and couldn't find Gwen's valuables. Obviously, we were upset. Finally, I went to move Gwen's empty suitcase and under it was Gwen's bag of valuables. It was a rough start to the trip. A drink at dinner helped get us back on track.

 The Greens, old friend of ours from San Francisco who had moved to London, picked us up for dinner. They drove us around a bit on our way to Cunningham's of Curzon Street, a Mayfair restaurant opened by London's "oyster king" in 1945. Our first views on the way were not disappointing. Gwen commented that the restaurant was sort of like those in New York, but more charming, with—as Gwen described it—its "tilting floors" and a very English atmosphere with banged-up pewter and no tablecloths. We had Lobster Cunningham that was very tasty but a small serving and a small salad. Stilton cheese finished the meal with good coffee, Turkish-style (quite thick). It was an exhausting day, but we were young. The next time we dined at Cunningham's, we had excellent roast beef served from a cart.

 The hearty English breakfast we had the next morning was wonderful, with tea that was the best we'd ever tasted. We were now ready to greet London and thought it was best to start with Tour #1. It stopped at the expected places, where I could explain to Gwen how things looked different from when I was there during the war. On this perfect day, Buckingham Palace and the Changing of the Guard ceremony, the Tower of London, and London Bridge looked "like a postcard." St. Paul's Cathedral, in all its glory, having survived the "blitz," showed off its beautiful new altar and was noted by Gwen to be quite baroque. Even nearly two decades after the World War II bombings, there were major gaps on city blocks that hadn't been filled in. Of course, we visited

The Old Curiosity Shop, which turned out to be very small and crowded. We finished our first full morning in London with lunch at Fortnum & Mason. It reminded Gwen of an elegant food store in San Francisco, Goldberg, Bowen & Co., only with carpet and chandeliers. We could not understand why waitresses looked surprised when we asked for more tea. We were obviously clueless about "tea time" in England. We crossed the street to The Burlington Arcade, where we bought cashmeres, then followed through to Old Bond Street with all its wonderful shops—all quite fun.

Gwen with a Beefeater guard at the Tower of London.

When we were on our morning tour watching The Changing of the Guard, we met a young man who was a student in London. He offered to drive us on a tour to Oxford for a reasonable fee, and we took him up on his offer. He picked us up the next morning in some sort of a small English car; it took us two hours to get to Oxford because of bad traffic. It was an overcast day, but we enjoyed our visit to Oxford, particularly the colleges, with their beautiful architecture and lovely green lawns in the center. We first visited Christ Church College. We then climbed the narrow stairs of the tower of Magdalene College, enjoying its lovely views of the square surrounded by other buildings of the college. The chapels were especially beautiful. We had lunch at a pub in Oxford, our first pub experience, and it was just what we expected of an English pub. It looked like it had been there for a long time, and the walls were covered with wood carvings. We had some good beer and sandwiches. On our way back, we passed Blenheim Palace, an imposing yet not very attractive mass, in our opinion. We stopped at Banbury Cross for some good cakes, then made a quick stop at Stonehenge. At the time of our visit, we were allowed to walk freely among those massive stones. It was difficult to imagine how these stones could have been placed so well at the time the structure was built. We found them to be more protected and less accessible on future visits. Before we left, it began to rain.

Gwen in front of prehistoric Stonehenge.

That day, we had agreed to meet an ex-patient of mine, Jean Johnson-Smith, who was now a friend, at Claridge's for tea at 5 p.m., which is why we had decided to take in Oxford in the morning. The traffic from Oxford back to London was impossible. We got to a phone and were able to reach Jean to tell her we would be late but that we were on our way. We got to Claridge's cold and wet. I went to the most elegant men's room I had ever seen and cleaned up a bit. We found Jean, who was lovely and gracious as always. She was a psychiatrist, and her husband had just been elected to Parliament. We went to Claridge's splendid lounge, where a gentleman in a tailcoat came to take our order once we were seated. I asked for tea. He replied that teatime had passed. I said surely I could have some hot tea in this most elegant hotel in England. He said not at this time of day. Can you imagine? (We were still clueless!) I settled for a Scotch, which *was* available. Jean told us she had arranged for us to visit Parliament a few days hence, which was to be quite a treat, since Mr. Churchill would be in attendance, probably for his last official appearance there. I had last seen Churchill when he, General Eisenhower, and General Patton had reviewed my unit on that day in June of 1944 in England just a couple of days before D-Day and our departure for France.

After our scheduled tour on our first full day in London, we decided that we should design our own daily tours going forward. Following another splendid breakfast the day after our Oxford excursion, we went to Westminster Abbey. We both delighted in seeing the names of so many whose works had contributed to our lives. I especially appreciated a window dedicated to the airmen who won "The Battle of Britain" and that cited their planes and names. We next visited Westminster Hall in the Parliament Building. Some days later, Jean took us to the visitors' gallery to hear Winston Churchill make his last speech in Parliament. He definitely sounded like

Winston and not some old tired warrior. The ovation he got was a tearjerker. Afterwards, we walked on Westminster Bridge and then continued to the Tate Gallery. It is hard for me to believe that we still had the energy afterward to go to Harrods for tea; Gwen felt it had a shabby look. Actually, all of London seemed shabby at that time. The city was obviously still recovering from World War II. Tea was accompanied by our first experience eating cucumber sandwiches.

    I had to leave Gwen during our first stay in London, because one night, while I was eating soup at the acclaimed Mirabelle restaurant, I had part of a tooth fall into the soup bowl. A London friend of mine, Gerald Sawyer, sent me to a dentist he knew, who worked for the National Health Service, where he did a temporary repair of my tooth. I was not charged, so I returned to give him a bottle of fine brandy. It became a family joke that I had broken a tooth while eating soup.

    Having to return to our hotel on her own that night, Gwen had fun using British money for the first time and finding her way back to the Mayfair district on the London Underground. She would not have done that when we revisited London in 2014, when we were both in our nineties.

    On another night, we had dinner at a restaurant called Scott's. Colchester oysters were followed by Sole à la Scott's (sole in a light cream sauce with shrimps and mushrooms)—all for about $7. After dinner, we saw a play, *Drop of a Hat*, at the Apollo, starring two talented British performers, Michael Flanders and Donald Swann. They sang humorous songs and had a funny patter like Mort Sahl. (It was much different from a play by the same name staged in San Francisco in 2014). Coffee was served at the intermission. We followed the play with dessert at the Savoy Grill, where we had fraises des bois ("strawberries of the woods") with Devonshire cream—wonderful! Gwen particularly liked the Savoy's elegant ladies room, the first such we had encountered in London. As she recalled, "It was spacious, clean, newly decorated, beautifully appointed. The Grill was less attractive."

A splendid touch we noted on this, our first visit to London, were the bright yellow flowers everywhere in window boxes and other containers on the dark old buildings still suffering from The War.

The next day we had to awaken early, much to our displeasure, as we had a long day ahead. We took a cab to Paddington Station, where we boarded a train bound for Slough—an odd name for a town, we thought. There we transferred to Windsor for the first of many subsequent visits. Of course, we saw the extraordinary Queen Mary's Dolls' House, the state apartments, St. George's Chapel, and the Albert Memorial. The Horseshoe Cloister had magnificent rooms and hundreds of famous paintings, including one room full of Van Dykes and another with paintings by Rubens, Holbein, Rembrandt, and others. We dropped in at the Windsor post office to buy stamps, which we never seemed to have enough of, before catching a bus that was just leaving for Hampton Court Palace.

Upon arrival at Hampton Court, we had a late lunch at The Mitre Inn—charming, very British, yet they did not have steak and kidney pie. We found Hampton Court more beautiful than anything we had seen. The handsome gardens were beautifully kept. The half of the building started by Cardinal Thomas Wolsey in the early 1500s and subsequently occupied by Henry VIII was Tudor style, and the other half, built by Christopher Wren for William II and Mary II in the late 1600s, was baroque style. We admired the paneling and wood carving by Grinling Gibbons, which was similar to what we had seen in many other important buildings. Here too there were magnificent paintings on display. We caught a bus that took us close to our hotel in London. The Greens picked us up once again to take us to The Players Club, a private club that provided a Victorian-era show mostly of sort-of-corny songs and accompanied by a nice dinner. We took a short walk on The Embankment and then headed home to our Mayfair lodgings. We could not believe how nice the Greens had been to us.

John on the grounds of Windsor Castle.

When Gwen and I first visited London, we found the cab fares to be especially low, but over the years, the fares became very high, so we switched to buses to get around and used them a great deal during later visits. That turned out to be fun, and the book of passes called an Oyster card was quite convenient.

On our first trip, there were still many bombed-out areas in the heart of London. Those that were under construction were being rebuilt in the original style. On later visits, there were new, more-modern buildings, but even then, there was an effort to conform to historical styles in most of central London.

Of course, we returned to London many times. On our second visit, we visited Churchill's bunker, now called the Churchill War Rooms, where Churchill and his war cabinet took shelter during World War II. At the time of that second visit, it had not changed since the war, and Churchill's "batman" (personal aide), who was still alive, led us on a wonderful tour that included many stories about the war. The bunker was rather crude, but it obviously did the job. Churchill's bed was not much more elegant than a cot, and there was a simple phone by it. The war room, of course, had maps with pins showing the location of troops, etc., as well as a number of phones in different colors.

On that outing, we also went to Dennis Severs' House, which was quite an adventure. Stanton Delaplane, a popular travel columnist for the *San Francisco Chronicle*, had recommended it. It's at 18 Folgate Street in a dismal part of London. Our cabdriver would not let us out of his sight until we were safely inside. The house is more than just a well-preserved domicile. It is a superb and intimate portrait of the lives of a family of Huguenot silk weavers, refugees from France, and whose history there stretches from 1724 to the twentieth century. Each room represents a different period of time and with that were the changes that occurred in the family's lives and the culture of the country. Each room looked lived-in, with such things as food and pipes of the time or newspapers on the table. There was a recorded broadcast for each room supplemented by the host. So we could follow the fortunes of the family through the generations: the sights, smells, and sounds of the house brought it all to life. It was Severs' intention with the house that, as one passed through this meticulously crafted world, it would be akin to exploring the surface of a painting with one's senses and imagination.

On my first trip with Gwen to London, I looked up the aforementioned Gerald Sawyer, who had been a classmate of mine when I was attending medical school at UC Berkeley in the 1940s. At a young age, he had become chief of endocrinology at the University College Hospital in London and was the very knight in shining armor who found me a dentist after the soup bowl incident. We'd reunite again and again on my subsequent trips to London. It was he who introduced us to The Connaught, the best hotel Gwen and I had ever stayed in. I returned there many times. When I invited him to come to Mount Zion Hospital in San Francisco as a guest professor, he in turn invited me back to London on a number of occasions to consult and speak at the University College Hospital. The highlight was when I was invited to be the principal speaker on Empire Day. When I began my talk on my work with Alan Margolis on erythroblastosis of the newborn, I showed some pictures of San Francisco I had taken. The chairman interrupted, saying, "Mr. Kerner, you have to stop this. We are already losing some of our best to you."

Regarding my numerous stays at The Connaught, eventually I was treated like visiting royalty, "comped" to suites and extended many courtesies, at least until a big chain took it over. On one occasion, I gave an elegant luncheon in our sitting room.

Gerald continued to be an excellent host. He and his wife drove us into the countryside on each visit. One of our most interesting excursions was to the Rothschild estate that is now a museum endowed by the family. Housed there were the art treasures that the European branch of the family sent to England to avoid having them confiscated by the Nazis. We also attended wonderful outdoor concerts with Gerald and his wife, given in the gardens of other great homes.

More about Gerald: he had come to UC Berkeley as a med student for a year while attending medical school in England. He was a great addition to our class, having come from a different world. In our senior play, he was perfectly cast acting as our professor of anatomy, John Bertrand de Cusance Morant Saunders, who later became dean and then chancellor. Saunders had a way of throwing chalk at sleeping students with amazing accuracy; he was a student of golf and the mechanism of hitting a golf ball; he acted out the formation of the peritoneum—all of which were open to perfect satire. Gerald died at an early age. I am sure he tried to do too much. He not only taught at the university, but he also did his share of work at the National Health Service while running a private practice on Harley Street. In addition, he edited a journal and wrote significant medical articles. He was a good friend and I miss him—especially whenever I return to London.

One of our most memorable stays at The Connaught was in 2001. On September 11, we were staying in a spacious suite with two bathrooms, two dressing rooms, and a large reception room (all of this for the price of a single room). Because of all flights being canceled due to the terrorist attacks on the World Trade Center in New York City and the Pentagon in Washington, DC, a good number of Americans were stranded in London, so I suggested to the hotel management that I could easily put up another couple in our suite. Management thanked me, but did not accept my offer.

Speaking of that tragic date, the next day Gwen and I walked over to the American embassy that was nearby. The entire block in front of the embassy was piled high with bouquets of flowers and notes of sympathy. That was so typical of the people of London, who still remembered and so appreciated our country's efforts in World War II.

CHAPTER TWO

Paris • 1958 / French Riviera • 1964

—*Paris*—

When we left London on our first trip bound for Paris, I was ill with a low-grade fever. I didn't want to tell Gwen, because I was sure she would want to go home. The flight to Paris was fifty-five minutes. Even though the flight was short and we were in "Tourist" class, lunch was served. Upon our arrival, we took a bus into Paris. It was a long ride, but we saw many of Paris's famous landmarks on the way in. Our hotel, the Hôtel de France et de Choiseul, on the Right Bank, seemed dumpy to Gwen, but it had a nice courtyard, and in retrospect, it had a good location near the Place Vendôme. It is still in operation.

I spent a good deal of time in Paris during World War II. I had won a trip there in a raffle after fighting in the Battle of the Bulge. At that time my unit had been in combat for about six months, and I was allowed to take a trip to Paris, which by then had been liberated. When the war was over, my unit ended up being stationed in Rheims, outside of Paris, waiting for possible deployment to Japan. During those six weeks, there was little for me to do; I had to work only half a day each week and spent the rest of the week exploring various parts of Paris.

So I could hardly wait to show Gwen around and at the same time visit some of my favorite spots. It came as a minor shock when we found everyone speaking French. Gwen had never been anywhere before where a foreign language was spoken, and this was a language she had studied at Lowell High School in San Francisco and at Stanford University. Gwen was pleased to find that everyone with whom we had to deal understood her

French. Joy! She was equally surprised that some people spoke English very well.

When we checked in to our hotel, I noted that across the street facing the Rue Saint-Honoré there was a restaurant, La Truite, advertising on its sign "Chicken on a String." I was still nursing my fever, and I thought if there is chicken there must be chicken soup. That sounded like a perfect treatment. It was dinnertime, so we cleaned up, unpacked minimally, and crossed the street to what turned out to be a charming, provincial-style restaurant. I still hadn't told Gwen that I was ill. Believe it or not, after a large bowl of perfect chicken soup and an otherwise simple meal, which included poulards sur ficelle, pommes, champignons, and Quincy vin (all costing $11.50, including tip), I began to feel better. They didn't teach me about chicken soup as therapy in med school, but Grandma knew best. After dinner we walked a bit on the Rue Saint-Honoré and the Place Vendôme. We knew we were in Paris. Gwen noted that the buildings were taller than in London, and the taxis were small. The bed was comfortable.

I was anxious to show Gwen how much I knew about Paris. We spent our first full day sightseeing. We walked to the Jeu de Paume. Up to that point in our lives, we had never seen such splendid examples of impressionist and postimpressionist art. It was too much to absorb in one visit. Over the years, we revisited that collection many times. We never got tired of those visits. Our last viewing of these masterpieces was in 2012, when we visited the splendid Musée d'Orsay, where most of the collection now resides.

Our first day in Paris, the weather was beautiful, so we walked through the Tuileries Garden to a Metro that we took to the Arc de Triomphe and its Tomb of the Unknown Soldier. Totally energized, we then went to the Eiffel Tower, which was even more impressive than we had expected; the views from the observation deck on that sparkling day were perfect and made it possible for us to understand better the layout of Paris. We went to a two-star restaurant, La Bourgogne, for lunch, a memorable meal. Gwen and I were used to small lunches. We ordered an omelette. The maître d', who spoke only French, said, "This is a two-star restaurant. That is not a proper order." It was expected of us to order several courses, plus wine and dessert and cheese. We said that we really wanted just an omelet and some wine. The omelet we got with cheese grated on it was the best we had ever had in our lives. There were also long, thin French rolls with sweet butter, along with a carafe of Beaujolais. The maître d' ended up comping us with dessert. The bill was about $7. *Sacré bleu!*

Gwen in front of the Eiffel Tower.

We returned via the Opera and had our first tea at the nearby Café de la Paix. On future visits, we would always see someone we knew while sitting at one of the café's sidewalk tables, but not this time. On the other hand, it was always a good spot for people-watching. Our first dinner in Paris was at Chez Mercier. Gwen described it as being like Jack's in San Francisco, "homey" but better. It was full. We enjoyed a meal of artichauts vinaigrettes, grilled sole, and parfait café, with "divine" little cookies. We passed on the evening coffee in favor of a good night's sleep. The vin de la maison was $5 a carafe. After dinner, we walked down the Champs-Élysées. The area was brightly lighted. We spotted the nightclub called SEXEY, where we knew that the brother-in-law of Pierre, an acquaintance of ours, worked. (We knew Pierre from San Francisco, where he been captain at Trader Vic's and then owned his own restaurant in Marin that was known for its perfect duck.) Pierre's brother-in-law proved to be a perfect host. He invited us back for a drink, but they would not be opening until later in the evening. This was the first time I heard Gwen engaged in a long conversation in French. She mentioned that every restaurant had a cover charge of usually 100 to 200 francs, up to a maximum of 400. We had already had quite a day, but we promised to return to the SEXEY on another night.

> **From Gwen's travel diary:** *Yes, all those famous things are really here!. . . .Nice friendly people, even the taxi man.. . . .Next concession to Paris: put eyeshadow all around the lid instead of just on the lash line.*

On our second day in Paris we rented a car. It was a Citroën 2CV. It had a canvas top that went back and forth like a window shade. The gearshift lever was a right-angled lever and of course, it was a stick shift. We called it "tout suite" ("as quickly as possible" in English), and it took a little getting used to. Since it was such a low-riding car, I couldn't see the road signs very easily, and at one point I was stopped by a gendarme for going through a stop sign that I didn't see. On the other hand, we discovered that in many places the authorities had actually lowered a lot of the road signs to accommodate the small, postwar, inefficient vehicles.

The Kerners' rented Citroën that they nicknamed "tout suite."

From Gwen's travel diary: *[Car] window falls down when door slams. Oh well. Nice driving. Paris driver's motto: NEVER stop for pedestrians. Otherwise, for all the confusion, everything seems to work very well.*

I can't believe that on our second day, we managed to drive our compact Citroën to Château de Malmaison, the beautiful home of Napoléon's mistress, located about thirteen miles west of the center of Paris. We admired the well-proportioned Regency interior and the beautiful, well-maintained grounds. The library was particularly stunning. We then drove to Montfort-l'Amaury, a favorite destination for my parents. Many elegant Parisians took their lady friends there for the weekend. The road then was narrow, but no problem for our little car. The place was quaint and charming. We decided that it was worth a return visit. We had lunch at Auberge de la Moutière, a really posh place with beautiful flower arrangements. The lunch consisted of four courses with good wine—all for just around $11! The specialty was an interesting omelette; we never could figure out what was in it, but it was delicious. I had a favorite for dessert: a superb tarte aux pomme.

We continued on to Versailles for the afternoon. We were both captivated by this remarkable palace and grounds.

> **From Gwen's travel diary**: *What a gigantic place! Some parts most impressive and lovely, some parts green canvas walls hung with portraits. In great apartments, some magnificent chandeliers. Down the Queen's staircase and into the Jardins. Acres and acres with fountains and walks. Some [fountains] needed repair and did not work. FINALLY, simple beautiful rain followed by bright sun. Next stop: the Petit Trianon.*

We returned to Paris and to Versailles many times over the years. Because of my being awarded the French Legion of Honor in Washington, DC, in 2007, we were invited to an elegant reception in the elegant Versailles Hall of Mirrors the next time we were in Paris. On that visit, we found the royal apartments restored to their former glory and all the fountains repaired. We made one more visit to Versailles during that Paris trip just to see the fountains all going at full flow.

Gwen in front of one of the fountains at Versailles, 1958.

Speaking of my Legion of Honor medal (see Chapter Fifteen), after I was given the honor, I would wear my medal whenever we were out and about during any of our frequent trips to Paris. I soon discovered that my little beribboned medal carried a bit of clout, and it opened my eyes as to how appreciative everyday Parisians were of my service during World War II.

On one of our more recent trips, there was a major exhibition of Matisse and Picasso. The first thing I did when we got there was to see if I could acquire tickets, but quickly discovered that the tickets were sold out for the entire show. The concierge said if we went early in the morning we might be able to get in. When we went to the museum early the next day, there was a line three to four people deep all the way around the block. We felt discouraged and knew we couldn't wait that long. But when we went to the main gate, the guard spotted my Legion of Honor ribbon and said, "Let me take you in. It would be an honor to have you visit here." So he escorted us in and introduced me to some of the museum staff. Not only were we given immediate entrance, but they also insisted that we not pay. It was a wonderful exhibit, incidentally.

John at Sacré-Cœur Basilica in the Montmartre district, 1958.

On another occasion, we were staying in a small hotel on the Rue Saint-Honoré. There was a really good hairdresser close to our hotel whom Gwen really liked. She was expensive but good. While Gwen was having her hair done, I went across the street to a busy train station to get tickets for the Metro. We would always get a special Carte 10 (a book of ten tickets), as we enjoyed taking the Metro in Paris; we found the French underground to be very efficient and much better than London's. In any event, when I arrived at the ticket office, the man selling the tickets saw my Legion of Honor ribbon. He wanted to know how I had gotten the ribbon, given that I was an American. I told him I fought in World War II to help liberate Paris. He then took it upon himself to take me around to several of the many shops in the underground to introduce me to everyone. He was very proud of the fact that I had been honored that way. The attention and heartfelt reaction were so unexpected. And it extended beyond the station. When we would ride the Metro, quite often little old ladies would get up and offer me their seat.

Years later, Lalique, the famous French glassmaker, had opened a hotel and restaurant across from the Musée d'Art Moderne de Paris, and we wanted to check out the restaurant. The dining room was quite elegant, and when I went up to the maître d' to make a reservation, he gave us a nice table after which he made a big deal about my Legion of Honor ribbon and was so pleased about my arrival that he introduced me to the entire restaurant staff.

On these later trips to Paris, with my ribbon pinned to my jacket, I got used to people on the street stopping me to thank me for helping them save their country from the Germans. And at restaurants, we often received a free glass of champagne or wine when the service staff spotted my Legion of Honor ribbon. It was always heartwarming and a bit bittersweet to experience the deep appreciation the people of Paris still felt toward Allied soldiers after all those years.

***

—French Riviera—

On one of our early trips to France, Gwen and I visited the French Riviera for the first time. We stayed at a small hotel by the water. One afternoon we heard screams of help in French. I ran out and saw a man lying on the ground not far from our room. He had walked through a glass wall and blood was spurting from his leg. Holding his leg, I had Gwen get a pressure bandage and as I put the bandage on the man's leg, Gwen called an ambulance. In the meantime, while we were trying to comfort the man, a local doctor arrived on the scene and put a tourniquet on the leg. I argued with him, insisting that he remove the tourniquet as it was cutting off all circulation, and I was afraid the injured man would lose his leg. I continued to argue with him and instructed the ambulance crew to remove the tourniquet, which they did. The vascular surgeon that the man's family had summoned to the hospital repaired the damaged vessel and agreed that the tourniquet might have caused the leg to die. That evening, as the man was in the hospital recovering, his family—an elegant group—was dining where Gwen and I were having dinner. I went over to check on the man with his family and as I approached their table, the women all stood up in honor of my saving their family member's leg. Indeed, I had preserved collateral circulation long enough to keep the leg alive until the surgeon could repair the leg. When we arrived back in our room, I found a thank-you note and a bottle of Cognac waiting, a gift from the man we helped rescue.

CHAPTER THREE

Venice • 1958

On our TWA flight to Venice, our next destination on our first grand tour of Europe, as we headed to a short layover in Geneva, our pilot made a turn around Mount Blanc, a courtesy rarely done these days. It was a crystal-clear day, and the Alps were magnificent. Gwen would have been happy if the pilot would have just continued on his way; she was not yet used to flying. In Geneva, since our flight to Milan was delayed, the airline treated all of the passengers to lunch at a charming, out-of-doors place. We sat down to a large, delicious dish of pasta accompanied by carafes of red wine. We thought that was lunch. However, the pasta was followed by a full meal with dessert! Before we took off again, we picked up a music box for our daughter, Jan. We were running about an hour late, but we did get seats in first class (very posh) to Venice, arriving at 7:30 p.m. From the Venice Marco Polo Airport, we transferred to the train that takes visitors the final leg to Venice proper.

> **From Gwen's travel diary**: *Magnificent flight to Geneva. Wonderful and clear day, you could see everything . . .*

From the train station, it was a few steps to the canal, where all kinds of boats were waiting for passengers. We chose a gondola. It was a perfect, balmy night with a full moon. We traveled along various canals. It was all so beautiful that we didn't want the gondola ride to end. Our hotel, the Regina (now the Westin Europa & Regina), faced the Grand Canal. We were greeted with flowers and letters. We never found out who sent the flowers, but I now suspect they were compliments of the hotel. Although we had arrived at a late hour, the hotel had saved dinner for us. When we finally arrived in our room, we walked out onto our room's large balcony, which looked over the canal and the lit-up Santa Maria della Salute cathedral directly across. All of that with a full moon made a heavenly scene one would expect on the perfect honeymoon.

*John on his room's balcony overlooking
the Grand Canal at the Regina hotel.*

Our hotel room was a sight we would never forget; whoever recommended it earned our undying gratitude. We returned there a number of times, most recently with our son Jim, his wife Sheryl, and our grandson Ryan. They took innumerable pictures from our balcony. Room #75 had a brand-new bathroom, which added to our pleasure in just being there. We had agreed to meet our good friends, Maury and Phyllis Baruch, who were also staying at our hotel. We walked around San Marco and selected a small restaurant where we could eat outdoors under a full moon. For all of us, it was in fact a fairy-tale city. We were so impressed, and it was so romantic.

Gwen having breakfast on their hotel room's balcony.

In all our many years and trips, we have never had such a glorious arrival as our first visit. In Venice, I switched from black-and-white film to the color film that was just beginning to be popular. I guess most travelers felt the way we did when they saw Venice for the first time. At that time, there was no scaffolding or crowds of tourists. Of course, we took in all the major sites. We visited the splendid St. Mark's Basilica on Piazza San Marco, where we got our first sight of the beautiful mosaics we were to see throughout Italy. We went to the top of the campanile. In 1902 the tower collapsed completely during repairs, but was carefully restored over a period of several years. At the top, we were treated to a splendid view. From there the city looked like a mass of orange-colored roofs. While we are taking in the view, bells start chiming, which gave the whole experience a particular charm. The Doge's Palace is a special place that has been restored since our first visit. On a later trip, we had a chance to see it after restoration, when it was even more glorious. With the walls lined with massive paintings and the marble floors and the gold decorations, the palace was quite a memorable sight.

The Doge's Palace on the Piazza San Marco (St. Mark's Square).

From Gwen's travel diary: *September 28, 1958, my first day in Venice. Beautiful sky this morning on the way to San Marco. [Visited] the cathedral while Mass was going on—a beautiful choir. The bells started chiming while we were there—WOW! At the Doge's Palace, the marble floors bounced when people walked. There are more gold decorations in this palace than one finds in the palaces in France . . .*

The dome of the basilica of Santa Maria della Salute as seen from the Kerners' hotel balcony.

We went to the Lido, where we viewed a palace called the Excelsior. On a later trip to Venice, we had the pleasure of visiting a palazzo, the home of a good friend of my mother's, the Countess Gozzi. She had been the owner of a factory that made the most beautiful material called Scalamandré. We had furniture upholstered in that material; it's now more than twenty years old, and it looks like new. An American interior designer named Elsie McNeill Lee, she married Count Gozzi after being a success in business. She provided most of the money, and he his name. Their palazzo had one room just to house the count's family silver. The palazzo had a splendid "flying" spiral staircase that was a triumph of engineering.

We had our first formal dinner in Italy at a restaurant overlooking the Piazza San Marco called the Caffè Quadri. We had the best cannelloni we'd ever eaten and scampi a la Quadri and meunière—all of this followed by baked almond ice cream meringue (Gwen: "very good!"). Including Soave white wine, the dinner cost us $10. A nightcap in the square with accordion music in the background was the perfect way to finish quite a day.

We were always asked to do things for family and friends when we traveled. My mom had asked us to order some tables while we were in Venice. Actually it was fun to conduct a bit of business. The big problem was communicating, but somehow we managed. We had gone to Italian language classes for about six months before leaving home. Whenever we visited Venice, we went to the Accademia di Belle Arti. The academy curators were always doing something to make their splendid collections of massive Venetian paintings more attractive. It is always overwhelming to see so many Tintorettos, Titians, Capriccios, and Veroneses in one place. My mother and father always stayed at the Gritti Palace, so on our first visit, Gwen and I went to the hotel for lunch the first chance we got. The setting is superb, with its deck right next to the Grand Canal. However, the food was only fair and the most expensive we had anywhere in Europe.

We returned to the Gritti Palace when my parents took our whole adult family there to celebrate their fiftieth wedding anniversary. At that time we had a corner room with a balcony and didn't worry about the cost. During that visit, one day I had breakfast alone with my father before the ladies were up. I asked my father what he planned to do that day. He said, "Today I bring wine to the gondoliers who ferry across the Grand Canal." Of course, I said I would like to join him. The ladies had shopping to do. He hired a large gondola and loaded it with small barrels of wine. We then rowed down the Grand Canal. At each gondola crossing, of which there were many, he left a keg of wine. As the gondola moved down the canal, the gondoliers who worked at the crossing points yelled "Kappy, Kappy." Kappy was my father's nickname. What fun! What a dad!

It was always pleasant to meet friends of my parents. In every city my mother had found someone to help her with purchases for her growing decorating business. One of these acquaintances of hers, Renato, proved to be the perfect guide in Venice. We went to the Ca d'Oro, a splendid palazzo with beautiful gold decorations. We always returned to shop on the Rialto Bridge. We learned that the best prices were nearby.

On our first trip to Venice, we began going to Harry's Bar. At that time, we would get two drinks and some little sandwiches for $3. The last time we were there, the service was quite a bit more than $3. On our first visit, after dinner we would hire a gondola and take a long ride through various canals. Now that too costs a hefty sum.

We began exploring the neighboring islands on our first visit, and over the years we returned to the islands we especially liked. One island, San Giorgio Maggiore, is home to a school and the Teatro Verde. The stage is set so there's a beautiful view of Venice as a backdrop. On our first trip, we found time to visit Murano and Torcello and returned to both many times since. In Murano we were disappointed with the glassblowing factory, where they were not interested in our watching the workers; rather, they wanted us in their shops. The same was true of the lace makers. Their prices were out of line, we thought. On the other hand, the island of Torcello was a pleasant surprise. There is a lovely restaurant there in a small hotel owned by Cipriani. The restaurant looks out on a lovely garden. It was very posh. After lunch, we visited a church nearby that was very old but well-cared for. There was also a shop owned by a friend of my mother's. From him we bought two golden seahorses that I still have. My mother had another old friend who retired to this island, and we had a chance to visit him on a subsequent visit.

On another trip to Venice, my mother took me to tea with friends of hers who had a beautiful home on the Grand Canal. During the visit, I was taken to a room with a huge collection of Etruscan gold, including models of chariots, masks, and various figures. In all the museums we were to visit over the years, we never saw anything that equaled this collection. The next time we were in Venice I wanted to show this collection to Gwen, but the family had hidden it somewhere. The elderly patriarch of the family had died, and his heirs did not want to have to pay inheritance taxes on their collection, taxes that are particularly high in Italy.

Gwen observed that there was a lovely custom in the hotels of Venice. The rooms always had fresh fruit and bowls of water to wash it in. She also noted that at the better restaurants the menus were in French.

We never tired of Venice, and we returned there at least six times. When the Regina was being refurbished, we stayed at other hotels. The Danieli was the best. We were treated regally there, because we were celebrating an important anniversary, and the manager liked us. Gwen and I had a way of trying to look at home wherever we were. One day on our way along the Grand Canal, an Asian couple asked if they could take our picture, mistaking us for Venetians.

Gwen feeding the famous pigeons of Piazza San Marco.

When we finally had to leave Venice on our first trip, the weather had turned bad, so that made it much easier for us to depart "La Serenissima." We headed to Florence by train. We left Venice at 10:50 a.m., arriving in Florence at 1:37 p.m. The train was called a *Rapido*—and it was.

CHAPTER FOUR

Florence • 1958

Upon our arrival in Florence, the hotel bus picked us up—a delightful service that we thought should be universal. The hotel was close to everything, and we had a nice view of the Arno River from our room, which was large and clean. Gwen especially liked the bathroom, which had "lots of plumbing" and was quite modern. We immediately went out and took a walk past the Palazzo Vecchio, with its magnificent staircase led by the standing Lion of Florence. We could see that there was much activity going on inside this cavernous palace. We learned that they were preparing for a meeting of prime ministers from various Mediterranean countries.

Our next stop was the splendid Duomo. We were impressed by its sheer size, the amazing dome, and the wonderful mosaics. The Baptistery was just across the way with its wonderful Ghiberti doors, which took the artist twenty-one years to complete. Bronze panels on the doors displayed stories from the Bible. We now have a copy of those doors in San Francisco in Grace Cathedral across the street from where I live—they are especially beautiful. The Baptistery's doors had been blackened from auto exhaust when we visited Florence the first time. They were later copied and these copies replaced the originals, which were moved to a museum behind the Duomo. Gwen made special note of Giotto's bell tower adjacent to the cathedral. We stopped for a drink and met a pleasant couple from New York. We walked to Harry's Bar, where we joined that couple for dinner. Tourists do that sort of thing, whereas it would be unlikely to do that at home. Dinner was good, and our tab was about $8. We walked them to their hotel, the Excelsior. It was more substantial than ours. My parents had stayed there, but we did not regret our choice. On another visit, we returned to the same hotel and the same room.

As we explored Florence, we had some difficulty finding our way around because of the narrow streets and sidewalks. However, one of the best parts about our first visit there was Gwen's knowledge about the city from her studies at Stanford.

Lorenzo Ghiberti's gilded bronze doors, the Gates of Paradise, *in the Piazza del Duomo.*

On this first visit to Florence we had a surprise experience. We managed to attend that major event honoring the prime ministers of the countries bordering the Mediterranean. Gwen and I were dressed in our best, having just dined at one of Florence's more elegant restaurants. As we were walking from dinner in the main square, we noticed that the Palazzo Vecchio was all lit up. As mentioned, we had been there earlier in the day, at which time we had seen workers preparing for something important. We approached the main entrance with its splendid stairway. The Lion of Florence had a wreath of flowers on his head. There were garlands of flowers all the way up the staircase. Gwen was reluctant to go in, but I thought we could do no harm, and since we were so well-dressed, we could easily pass as guests. No one stopped us as we climbed the stairs. The town hall, which is usually quite austere, was alight with indirect lighting and candles. There were elegant buffets at various points, and there was music. Gwen would not let me touch anything. We wandered around and observed all the elegant people. We noted how much more beautiful the palace was under these circumstances. Reluctantly, we left the event to return to our hotel.

    One of the highlights of our stay in Florence was a visit with my cousin, John, and his wife, who was a baroness, a native of Florence and a Catholic. The baroness offered to take us on a tour of the city. We had always considered the cathedral in the Piazza del Duomo as being the foremost church in Florence, but on this day, she took us to her favorite cathedral. Our visit was in the spring near Easter, so there was a good deal of pomp and ceremony going on in Florence's hundred-plus churches. In this church, as in most, there was a bank of candles that people lit to honor their loved ones or make a plea, after paying a coin. It was Passover, our Jewish religious holiday that coincides with Easter and was an important holiday during the time of Jesus. (In fact, the Last Supper was a seder.) So I approached this bank of candles, put my coins in the jar, and lit a candle. The candle began burning brightly, but after I said my Jewish prayer, the candle promptly went out. I thought, "Well, that's kind of funny." But then it was a Catholic church, after all.

The tower of the Palazzo Vecchio, Florence's town hall, built in 1314.

We had yet another memorable experience. A man with whom my mother had worked offered to drive us to the seashore. On the way, he picked up an attractive woman. When Gwen had assumed and indicated in poor Italian that the woman was his wife, we were told, amidst much laughter, that she was his "lady." He took us to a wonderful seafood restaurant at the shore. I could not believe what his lady friend ate. She started with a large bowl of mussels. Then she had a whole meal of pasta, and then fish, and of course, dessert. Our seaside excursion was a great chance for us to use the little Italian we knew. It was a very good day.

On our early trips to Florence, we could visit any of the top galleries simply by going to the entrance and buying a ticket. On our last visit, one had to have an appointment or go with a group that had a fixed appointment. Somehow that took away some of the pleasure of our early visits, especially to the Uffizi Gallery, which is overwhelming with its collection and certainly one of the best in the world. The way the paintings are displayed with a simple white background enhances their splendor. We were particularly drawn to Botticelli's *Birth of Venus*, which Gwen called "most lyrical and delicate." I believe they got up the nerve to send it to the Golden Gate International Exposition in San Francisco in 1939. Now they would not let it go anywhere except where it has resided for so many centuries. At the Uffizi, we also got our first taste, face to face, of Caravaggio. His *Bacchus* reminded Gwen of Édouard Manet. We were amazed at the large number of Rubens paintings.

All this culture was followed by a lovely lunch of clubhouse sandwiches at Harry's Bar, with a bill of $5. We then went to take a more careful look at the wonderful sculptures, most notably the statue of Perseus, in the magnificent, towering outdoor arched gallery, the Loggia della Signoria.

The chief surgeon in San Gimignano (with its five wonderful towers) was a doctor who had gotten some of his training in San Francisco in my department. He had grown up in Florence, and he and his wife wanted to show us around. He knew every bit of the history and anatomy of Florence. He knew who the artists were in every part of the Duomo. He pointed out the signature that the architect of the Loggia had carved in the far wall in small letters. Finally, his wife said that was enough. They took us to their favorite restaurant, where he said that he would order and that we should not ask what we were eating. It was an excellent meal in a simple yet elegant place. After enjoying a meal with a very good main dish and very good wine, we found out that our entree was rabbit. We had never eaten rabbit before.

Gwen at the Palazzo Vecchio tower with its clock, Florence's first public clock, installed in 1353.

Dining in Florence was hit and miss. My mother had recommended Villa La Massa as a top restaurant. It was elegant and expensive, but the food was not very good. Everyone there, however, spoke perfect English.

We also learned that a specialty of Florence was a T-bone steak, and we thought the steaks very good indeed. We found Florence, for all its beauty, to be a noisy place. There were an unbelievable number of motor scooters, and there were always church bells ringing.

One of the wonderful things that happened to us in our travels in Europe was that, in almost every city we visited on our early trips, we met up with friends of my mother and father. Bernard Berenson, the famous art historian, had a villa a bit outside Florence called the Villa I Tatti. There were tours available of the villa and Berenson's collection, but they were quite exclusive, so on a later visit to Florence, we arranged a visit to the villa through the Italian consul general in San Francisco. The group was made up of my mother, Gwen and me, and another couple. The woman who was now curator invited us to tea. I believe she was Berenson's mistress. She was charming and told us how Berenson acquired his most valuable painting. When he was young, he bought the painting because of its splendid frame. Years later, when he became a world-famous collector and advisor to top collectors, he found that the painting in that frame was the most valuable piece in his personal collection. There was a wing in the villa that housed his collection. He willed the entire property to Harvard University shortly before our visit. The grounds too were especially lovely, with the tall pines carefully placed.

Another acquaintance of my mother's, Giorgio Ciolli, took us, in a single day, to a number of places that might otherwise would have been difficult for us to find, including the Piazzale Michelangelo, with its splendid views; La Galleria dell'Accademia, with Michelangelo's breathtaking *David* along with his *Slaves*, which appeared unfinished (on returns visits to Florence, we always went back to this wonderful place); and the town of Fiesole, which boasts the best view of Florence. And we did all this before lunch!

Giorgio, his cousin, Guido, and Guido's "lady" took us to Pisa, with a brief stop at Terme di Montecatini, where there is a famous spa. My mother and father often ended their trips to Europe here to rest up for the trip home. It was also close to Florence, a city my mother loved. Lucca was also on our route. We thought the area quite resembled the Napa Valley, with the exception of the tall towers on hilltops and the Italian-style homes. This was the first area where we saw classic Roman ruins. In Pisa, the Leaning Tower was more beautiful than we expected, standing in its carefully tended grass setting. The first efforts at bracing the towers had just been put in place, so we could walk up a short way to get a good view of the neighboring cathedral. On later visits, thanks to elaborate efforts of engineering, the support system was less in evidence.

Pisa's main cathedral and baptistery are not talked about much, but they have their own particular beauty. The baptistery has a lovely dome, and the doors have elegant carvings. We were surprised to find the interiors of both spacious, with good lighting from the outside. Gwen, who always prided herself on her knowledge of architecture, was surprised that the inside of the church was so high and delicate and that it was Romanesque rather than Renaissance. On our return to Florence, we went to Sabatini, a popular restaurant that was crowded, but with only fair food, Gwen noted. The dinner was $6.

The next day we went to the Pitti Palace and the Boboli Gardens. The Pitti Palace was a surprise. Its silver gallery was splendid, as were its Medici jewelry and some impressive Titians (e.g., *Man with a Glove*). Elsewhere, there were many Raphaels. There, for the first time, we saw beautiful tables with elaborate inlaid patterns. On our first visit to the Boboli Gardens, they were rundown. The war was still having its effects, and major efforts to attract tourists were focused on the city's art displays. During this first trip, we often used a horse and carriage, which was a rare form of transportation in later years.

The Leaning Tower of Pisa, begun in 1173 and completed in 1372.

One of our friends, or perhaps my mother, had suggested we visit a store called Gucci. It was a small, one-of-a-kind shop. There was a nice man's wallet for sale for around $10. So for Christmas, I ordered a bunch of those wallets, all wrapped individually with Gucci paper, for my closest men friends. I knew they would enjoy them, because the leather was such high quality and would hold up for years. My wallet gifts were a big hit, even though no one knew anything about the Gucci brand at the time. Of course, today Gucci is known all over the world for its fine leather products.

Gwen and I always loved movies. In Italy we found that American films often had the sound dubbed in Italian or sometimes the movie was in English with subtitles in Italian. The former was more common. American movies were popular and predominant when we first went to Italy, but later we found that more films were being made in Italy.

On our last night in Florence on our first trip there was a huge fireworks display. Why we didn't know. We liked fireworks, and we found that they seemed to be coming up in our lives frequently.

On our last morning in Florence we went to the Medici Chapel (which had been closed). Its walls were covered in marble and semiprecious stones. Michelangelo had designed all of this splendor. There were elegant tombs for members of the Medici family designed by him. It was a good place to end our first visit to Florence. Now it was on to Rome, the Eternal City.

CHAPTER FIVE

Rome • 1958 / Lake Como • 1991

—*Rome*—

We took a nonstop train from Florence to Rome. Because there was no one to help us, we took our luggage ourselves to the baggage car and were given receipts for it. On this trip, there was no problem doing that. Because it worked so well, the second time we traveled by train to Rome we did the same thing. However, there was a delay getting our second case (Gwen's). When we finally got to our hotel, Gwen began unpacking and noted that the suitcase was neatly packed but HER JEWELRY WAS NOT THERE. We rushed back to the train station and reported the theft to the police. There followed a terrible interchange with the English-speaking police officer. We told him that the train was still in the station. Rather than call the station, he spent almost an hour quizzing us. He looked at our passports, asked our grandmothers' names, etc. He said that often things people had had stolen would end up being sold on the Spanish Steps. Essentially he did nothing, but I insisted that he give a written report. Fortunately, everything was insured, but some of the jewelry had irreplaceable sentimental value. We learned a big lesson then, which was to either leave all valuables home or carry them with you. Essentially, the police did nothing but drive us crazy. How I saved the day will come later.

Again, on our first trip, there was no such problem. The worst of it was a long delay at the Florence train station. (Ironic, as we had always heard that Mussolini had the trains running on time!). Once underway, the train trip was pleasant, because we met fellow travelers from Connecticut, who joined us for lunch. Upon our arrival in Rome, we found our way to the Pensione Pfister, which had been recommended to us. It was a small, old place at the top of the Spanish Steps. We were given a large room with a large balcony overlooking the Spanish Steps and a major portion of Rome. There were flowers awaiting us from a friend of my mother's. Breakfast was to be served on the balcony. We had our own small bathroom with a shower, but the toilet was down the hall. All of this was for an absurdly small amount of money. We returned to this place a number of times. It was across from the Hassler Roma, a very posh hotel. I got to know the concierge there because my parents were regulars. So, he gave me the daily newspaper and made reservations for me. He was a big help.

Ruins of the Circus Maximus, a sixth-century-BCE stadium where Roman chariot races were held.

  Almost immediately we went down the Spanish Steps to the posh Via Condotti, a fashionable street in the heart of Rome, where we bought a beautiful tortoise fitted clutch. Gwen always felt that Florence was more pleasant than Rome, but I loved the Eternal City. The weather was balmy, so we ate our first dinner at Fagiona, which had a loggia facing a large square, the Piazza Colonna. Dinner for two with wine was $7.

> **From Gwen's travel diary**: *In Florence, we had to WAIT AGES for the train. All roads lead to Rome—but some very slowly. . . . When we arrived at our hotel in Rome, we were met with a fisheye at the door. It took three minutes before the woman on the other side of the door figured out who we were. . . . Rome is the busiest place so far. Unbelievable traffic, pedestrians have no rights. Crossing the street is a real adventure.*

Close-up of St Peter's Basilica, designed by Buonarroti Michelangelo.

On our first visit to Rome, we took a bus tour. It covered some splendid sights, but, once again, we decided that group tours were not for us. We decided to rent a car instead, which was brave in that wild city, but we wanted the freedom. We rented a tiny Fiat that could be parked at right angles to the curb. Our first tour took us to the Vatican Museum and the Sistine Chapel, by several piazzas, and over the Tiber. Gwen found the Vatican Museum beautifully cared for but "not exciting." At that time, the Sistine Chapel had been "restored" a number of times, and essentially the ceiling and *The Last Judgment* had been spoiled. On a much later visit, the ceiling had been properly restored, and it proved to be breathtaking.

Our first lunch in Rome was at the Hassler Roof, a favorite of my mother's. It was posh but disappointing, with a price of $7, which was quite a bit; at that time we were paying about $8 a day for our room with breakfast. While at lunch, we spotted our rabbi from San Francisco, Alvin Fine, and his wife, Liz, and had a pleasant chat. We had begun to see people we knew as we traveled. Tourists then tended to go to the same places. In later years, tourists preferred to go to "out-of-the-way places," I think, in part, in wanting to one-up their friends.

On our first trip to Rome, we ventured out to nearby Tivoli to tour the Villa d'Este, a sprawling, sixteenth-century villa with exquisite terraced gardens and numerous elaborate fountains. It was the perfect spot for a picnic.

A view from the Tivoli Gardens, just outside Rome.

***

—Lake Como—

Over the years, Gwen and I kept hearing what a beautiful body of water Lake Como was, so in 1991 we decided we would go and stay in Bellagio. Shortly before we were to go on our trip, I had an operation on my left shoulder's rotary cuff, but we decided to go on the trip anyway, even though I couldn't use my left arm very well. When we got to the airport in Milan, the flights to Lake Como had been canceled, so we got tickets to take the two-hour train trip from Milan to the main station in Lake Como. Our comfortable compartment had a place above to store our suitcases. Because of my shoulder surgery, I couldn't lift them, so two men in our compartment helped me put them up above and refused tips. When we got to the station in Lake Como, I went to check my wallet that had my travelers' checks and passport, and it was gone, along with some of my ID. I always wondered, was it those two men who had assisted me with my luggage? As soon as we got to our hotel in Bellagio, we called the US embassy about the passport and then the American Express office about the travelers' checks.

American Express informed us that we would have to go back to the US embassy in Milan to get a new passport. The next day I left Gwen at our hotel and took the train back to Milan. Although the train from Bellagio to Milan was sold out, I got on anyway and sat in the lounge. No one asked me for a ticket. Once I got to the embassy in Milan, there was a long line waiting for services. I told them what had happened to me, and they put me to the head of the line. In less than two hours I had a brand-new passport. It all happened so quickly because I had a copy with me of the passport, something I always do when I travel.

After taking the train back to Bellagio, I found Gwen wandering around the town sightseeing. That night at dinner a man from American Express came to our hotel with $2,000 worth of travelers' checks for me. He told me that some million lira (approximately $870) of the stolen travelers' checks had already been spent. He bought us a nice dinner, and we were finally able to relax and enjoy our stay in Lake Como. The adventures of traveling!

CHAPTER SIX

Ireland • 1993

When I enrolled at the University of California at Berkeley as an undergraduate, I chose English as my premedical major. My interest was in drama, and I was particularly attracted to Irish literature, so this fueled my desire to visit the Emerald Isle with Gwen. We finally made it to Ireland in 1993, flying there on a flight from San Francisco via London.

> **From Gwen's travel diary**: *Auspicious beginning: driver on time, no traffic to airport. John asked if business class allowed us into the Red Carpet Lounge. YES! I get two drink tickets. It is now 5 PM and I am sold on business class. The seats are bigger. They call you by your name, [offer] free booze, [and have] table napkins. I like it.*

Once in Ireland, we signed up for a tour with a small group of people, and our first stop was the market town of Ennis in County Clare, where we were given Room 107 in the charming Old Ground Hotel. While there, we went on a tour of nearby Knappogue Castle, where we attended its grand and elegant medieval banquet and show.

On the first day of the tour, the tour director came to me. She knew I was an OB-GYN doctor, and she said one of the women on the tour would have to modify her travel because of a female problem. Many doctors don't want to get involved in medical issues when they're on vacation, but I wanted to try to help her. The director of the tour explained that the woman had a prolapsed uterus, and it was causing her discomfort. This meant that a portion of her uterus was protruding out of her vagina. This can cause any number of problems.

So, feeling empathy for the woman, I said I would be happy to talk to her and possibly help her with a simple device I had used before in similar situations called a pessary. It's a small circular device coated in silicon, and when you squeeze it and insert it in the vagina, it holds the fallen uterus in place so that surgery is not needed. They have been used since ancient times. The woman said she was willing to try the device so she wouldn't have to cut her trip short, and we found out that a pharmacy near us might have a suitable device. We were able to get the pessary, and I showed her how it use it and clean it. She was so relieved and grateful. After that event, the tour director made sure that Gwen and I had the best accommodations at every place we stayed!

The next portion of our trip was the rugged west coast of Ireland called the "Wild Atlantic Way" that runs some 1,600 miles from the Cliffs of Moher in County Clare to the Inishowen Peninsula in County Donegal, the northernmost county of Ireland. It was the most rugged coastline I've ever seen, and we have some pretty rugged coastlines in California. It looked like it had broken off of some other land mass in prehistoric times.

While touring this region, we visited the amazing Gregans Castle Hotel, which was also our lodgings. We were given a large suite that had a sitting room with a sofa and *two* bathtubs in the bathroom. We could have both taken separate baths at the same time! The floors were heated, most likely with circulating warm water. It was quite luxurious.

> **From Gwen's travel diary**: *Sept. 1, 1993:*
> *It's my birthday and John gave me a beautiful Amber necklace. We had breakfast in our private sitting room.*

We eventually made it to the capital of Ireland, Dublin. Gwen and I loved the beautiful eighteenth-century Trinity College Library, with its legendary "Book of Kells," a ninth-century illustrated Gospel book in Latin, famous around the world. There is a two-story-high, arched hall of the library called the "Long Room," with 200,000 of the library's oldest books kept in oak bookcases. It is truly magnificent. The main aisle is lined with busts of notable intellectuals.

Knowth, a Neolithic passage grave built some 5,000 years ago.

We took a side trip near Dublin to the Knowth mound. It was built around 3200 BCE. It's a large, grass-covered burial mound similar to the one in Newgrange near the River Boyne. We learned that there was a settlement there in 4000 BCE, and among its residents were great astronomers. There are many fascinating drawings inside this structure. It is said to be older than the pyramids and Stonehenge, and it houses the oldest-known drawing of the moon.

I mentioned earlier that I was attracted to Ireland because of my love of Irish literature and plays. We had the pleasure of going to two plays in Dublin put on by the Dublin Players. The plays dealt with The Troubles—the problems between Protestants and Catholics that the general public could relate to and sadly still exist in Ireland today. The Abbey Theatre is the national theater of Ireland and was founded in 1904 by W.B. Yeats and Lady Gregory. Its intent is "to bring to the stage the deeper emotions of Ireland." We really enjoyed those plays.

We also went to a large Irish products emporium, the Skellig Gift Store. Gwen bought a beautiful Irish tweed jacket, and I bought a warm jacket that I still have. These fabrics were especially designed for the cold, wet climate of Ireland.

Dublin is renowned for its pubs. Gwen and I usually went to a pub for lunch, opting for the specials of the day, usually sandwiches and soups, and a Guinness Stout, the national beer of Ireland. We enjoyed the architecture of the pubs, all very different and unique. The pubs were centers of social interaction in each part of town. They were just as charming as we had imagined, and the food was wholesome, with hearty breads.

Lovely Lough Leane in County Killarney.

From Gwen's travel diary: *After visiting the Waterford factory and Blarney Castle, we traveled by road over mountains with heather and grouse to the Park Hotel in Kenmare. We have the best room there overlooking the garden—sitting room, posh bathrobes, Irish breakfast in the room the next morning (orange juice, scrambled eggs, sausage, scones, toast and ham—heavenly!). We don't leave the hotel until 1 PM.*

Gwen and John about to take a carriage ride outside Muckross House.

We ended our tour of the Emerald Isle with a stay at the glamorous Muckross House in Killarney National Park. It looks out on the Muckross Lake, admired the world over for its striking beauty. We toured the massive house and imagined what it would have been like to live there—a Downton Abbey kind of life, no doubt. There was space in the lower level for servants, and we heard that Queen Victoria visited there in 1861 and that special furniture was made for her visit. Gwen and I had a ride in a horse-drawn carriage before retiring to our beautiful room. The master bedroom had two queen-size beds, and Gwen and I had to decide which bed we were going to sleep in.

    I guess the main thing I remember about Ireland was that we felt so relaxed there. We really felt like we were on a romantic trip together. The only thing that was even its equal was the first night we spent in Venice on our first trip to Europe; it was so beautiful and romantic that it was the kind of environment we would expect for a honeymoon night. We had that same feeling in Ireland—a beautiful setting for a lovely night together. The perfect place for a husband and wife away from their family on the beautiful Emerald Island.

CHAPTER SEVEN

Berlin • 2001

When I was going to high school, we were required to study a foreign language, and I chose German. I already knew I wanted to be a doctor, and I knew that the best modern research was being done in Vienna and Berlin. My father said I was crazy, that I should have studied Spanish because it was the second language of my home state, California. But I persisted and took German. When I went to college at Berkeley, I was required to take three years of language to study premed, so I signed up for scientific German. I was sad to find out that there wasn't much about the science of medicine in this class. I got my only D in medical school in German. Most of the students in my class were German refugees, and they enrolled in the class because they wanted a good grade for their records. So, it was hard for me to compete with fluent German speakers.

    Years later in Normandy shortly after D-Day, for the first time in my life I heard German being spoken as an everyday language. At night we could hear the German soldiers talking, we were that close to their camps. I and the group of eight men I commanded would pick up any wounded German soldiers we came upon and take them away to receive the care they needed. As a doctor I felt it was my duty to look after all human beings, even though I knew what the German high command was doing to the Jews. Later on in the war, when we invaded Germany, I was elected to speak to the mayors of the cities as we approached them, since I was the only one in our unit who spoke German. Although my German got better as the war went on, it was never very good. To this day, I still have a basic hatred of the Germans of the 1940s for what was going on with the Jews in the concentration camps.

During my tour of duty in Europe, I was always afraid of being captured, since I was Jewish.

After the war, when my mother took Gwen and me on a trip to Europe, we stopped in Hamburg, Germany, and I was able to use my German again. I was so impressed with the rebuilding they had done, I found myself softening my attitude toward Germany. The people I met in Hamburg after the war were friendly and, as the Cold War was now in full swing, they told us they would gladly join us against the Russians, if necessary.

It took me a long time to decide to go to Berlin, but after reading accounts about how interesting Berlin was, I considered going there with Gwen. By the year 2001, both Gwen and I concluded we were curious to see firsthand the great things that Berlin had to offer. We had time to study before we went and collected information about Berlin.

Gwen and John cuddle up to a sculpture of a bear, Berlin's mascot.

I was helped in planning our trip by a young man who was the son of one of my patients and had been a pilot in the US Army. He helped deliver food to Berliners during the Berlin Airlift in the late 1940s, when the Russians had blocked all surface access to the Western sector of Berlin. Our lodgings in Berlin were at a recommended hotel not far from the Brandenburg Gate near the Pariser Platz. The massive gate was built in the late eighteenth century by Prussian King Frederick William II and, given its close proximity to our hotel, Gwen and I thought it was the ideal place to start our exploration of Berlin.

We were impressed with the rebuilding the Germans had done in the area, restoring buildings carefully to their previous condition rather than tearing them down. Gwen and I decided to walk the length of the street from in front of the Gate to two of the great museums on Museum Island in Berlin. Along the way, as we passed a string of beautifully restored shops, Gwen spotted a dress on a mannequin in a window that she fancied, so we went in and bought it. It's a dress she kept all her life. We also passed a nice-looking French restaurant, Margaux, the only French restaurant in the area, so we stopped in and made a reservation to eat there on Gwen's upcoming birthday, French food being her favorite cuisine.

As we continued our walk, we decided after getting an initial look at the city that we would return another day to take in those two museums, and we headed back to our hotel. By now we had seen enough to know what we wanted to see. We were well aware of the German people's interest in the arts and were impressed that their museums had art from all the classic periods, from ancient times up the current day.

On our list of museums to visit was the Pergamon Museum. We were already somewhat familiar with the museum, because we'd seen the famous Pergamon Altar in an exhibit in San Francisco. The money raised by that exhibit was to be used to improve the museum in Berlin. The altar is a massive, second-century-BCE structure reconstructed from ruins excavated by a German engineer in the ancient Greek city of Pergamon in Asia Minor in the late 1800s. It was impressive to think that the Germans transported the altar to Berlin so long ago. Another of the museum's treasures is the Ishtar Gate, from sixth-century-BCE Babylon. The museum had recreated the missing parts of the gate, and we found the reconstruction with its blue tile mind-boggling.

A small portion of the 2nd-century-BCE Pergamon Altar at the Pergamon Museum.

We also visited the Neues Museum, with its vast collection of Egyptian artifacts. One of the museum's major pieces is the bust of Nefertiti, sculpted in 1345 BCE (at the time of our visit, the bust was being housed at the Egyptian Museum in Berlin's Charlottenburg borough).

Both of these museums on Berlin's Museum Island have very impressive Greek and Roman collections. The fact that these magnificent items were taken from their countries of origin is disturbing to many. There was disunion about returning them to their rightful countries, not unlike the controversy surrounding the Elgin Marbles in the British Museum that were taken from the façade of the Parthenon in Athens, Greece, in the early 1800s. It was a time when the English, French, and Germans were competing for major artifacts from the Middle East for their museums.

> **From Gwen's travel diary**: *Sept. 1, 2001: The next morning we walked over to the Potsdamer Platz shopping street and had a snack in the basement of the Galerie Lafayette. Next the Pergamon Museum, which is excellent, but not in good repair. We took a pedicab back to our hotel. 7 pm birthday dinner at the Margaux, very pretty, delicate food. It was hard to find a cab back to our hotel, but it was a good birthday.*

Even though I was using my German on this trip, I still found it difficult to speak the language, because it always reminds me of the Holocaust. During World War II, however, my German gradually improved, and I got more comfortable speaking it. After the war, when I was stationed in Koblenz, Germany, checking out the people returning home and delousing them when necessary, I became enamored with a German nurse who worked for me. She really caught my attention, and I seriously considered marrying her, but I thought bringing her back to the

United States might be difficult, so I eventually ended the relationship.

Returning to our hotel after our visit to Museum Island, Gwen and I made reservations to be taken privately to Potsdam and the Sanssouci Palace, where the peace plan was drawn up near the end World War II. Most of the area around Potsdam was still intact after the war. The Germans restored any of the buildings that were damaged to be as close to the originals as possible. Gwen and I were constantly being impressed, throughout our trip, that they were able to accomplish that.

A young man we met took us on a tour of Berlin, and we visited one of the most famous department stores in the world, KaDeWe (short for Kaufhaus des Westens, or Department Store of the West). The department store, founded in 1907 by a German Jew, is the second-largest one in Europe after Harrods in London. There are seven floors, and on the sixth floor is a food court where we came upon an amazing array of sausages. We didn't really care for sausages, but the display was very impressive.

Another excursion we greatly enjoyed was a ride aboard the *Mitte* on the Spree River, which flows through the heart of Berlin. We rode on the top deck near the front of the ship, where we could see the whole city and the countryside. The boat made stops around the city so we could get off and on.

We next stopped at Checkpoint Charlie, the America entrance to the former East Berlin at the Berlin Wall. By the time we visited there, most of the wall was gone. The remaining parts of the wall were covered with graffiti. We brought home an actual piece of the wall. We also visited the nearby Escape Museum, which displayed many of the crazy ways trapped Germans in East Berlin tried to escape. They built all kinds of homemade aircraft to help them fly over the wall. One escape mechanism was made with balloons that would hopefully lift them up over the wall.

Interior of the Reichstag, home to Germany's lower house of parliament.

We found a number of interesting places to eat in Berlin. We had tried to get into the government building, the Reichstag, in the main plaza, to go on a tour of it, but there was such a long line that we decided to make a dinner reservation at a restaurant inside the building. It was a good move. The reservation got us into this beautifully restored building. The Nazis tried to set it on fire in 1933 to get support for its party internationally, but the burning failed to garner it support. We found the Reichstag reminiscent of some of the great buildings in France. It seemed to us that the Germans were competing with the French when it came to great architecture. When Gwen and I saw photos of the buildings destroyed during World War II and how they look now, we thought that the United States could take a lesson from the restoration of Europe and shore up our own infrastructure and protect our architectural heritage.

The most difficult thing for me and probably for most other Westerners to reconcile is how the Germans could carefully restore their old architecture, and how much they love fine classical music and respect fine art, yet could have systematically killed millions. It was beyond our understanding. Today, Berlin has two first-rate symphonies, and they often played the music of Jewish composers.

Gwen and I visited the concentration camp at Auschwitz, and even though the people who operate it now have cleaned it up and have made it look less horrible, it was still horrid. We felt awful. Despite the horrors of the Holocaust, the amazing thing is that there are many pieces of sculpture in the Berlin area today devoted to the memory of the Jews who were killed during World War II, including a giant sculpture to memorialize the death of Jews during that tragic time. I found it interesting that there are major reminders for the German people about the Holocaust, particularly at the museums. The dramatic exhibits and displays are quite effective in creating a mood that recaptures the horrors of the Holocaust. When we were there in 2003, a monument was being built one block south of the Brandenburg Gate. The Memorial to the Murdered Jews of Europe consists of 2,711 concrete slabs arranged in a grid pattern over an area of 200,000 square feet. Underneath the undulating concrete slabs lies the museum—a powerful reminder of the horrendous treatment given the Jews, gypsies, the disabled, homosexuals, political opponents, and other groups during World War II.

War is a terrible way to settle disagreements. I know that men and many species of animals resort to violence when faced with conflict or a threat to their survival. After witnessing and surviving the horrors of Omaha Beach and the Battle of the Bulge, I believe more than ever that humans must learn a better way to settle major controversies. I understand why President Roosevelt tried initially to avoid our country's involvement in World War II. My feelings about war are pretty much summed up by the words he spoke in his famous "I hate war" speech, which he gave in Chautauqua, New York, on August 14, 1936, and has been immortalized on the walls of the World War II memorial in Washington, DC:

> *I have seen war.*
> *I have seen war on land and sea.*
> *I have seen blood running from the wounded.*
> *I have seen men coughing out their gassed lungs.*
> *I have seen the dead in the mud.*
> *I have seen cities destroyed.*
> *I have seen two hundred limping, exhausted men come out of line—the survivors of a regiment of one thousand that went forward forty-eight hours before.*
> *I have seen children starving.*
> *I have seen the agony of mothers and wives.*
> *I hate war.*

CHAPTER EIGHT

Africa:
Kenya, Zimbabwe, and Botswana • 1977 / Egypt • 1980

—*Kenya*—

By 1977, I had developed an interest in wild animals. I guess it was my frequent trips to the San Francisco Zoo. (My daughter, Jan, went so often she had learned the favorite foods of the various inhabitants.) In any event, I made reservations for Gwen and me to travel to Kenya. I practiced animal photography on our dog, Tasha, before our departure.

> **From Gwen's travel diary**: *We arrived at Keekorok Lodge at 5:20 PM. Cool!! Countryside lush, trees and valley very green. Our room overlooks the waterhole! That night, there they are... waterbucks! By 10 PM, we have seen rhinos, giant bush pigs, white-tailed mongeese, bushbucks.*

Upon our arrival in Kenya, the first place of interest we were taken was a Maasai Mara village. The women wore colorful bead necklaces (I bought one), and the men carried weapons (I did not buy one!). Interestingly, there was a large group of men who were unusually tall, almost seven feet. We continued on to the Keekorok Lodge, which sits right in the middle of the migrating animals. The lodge was magnificent and made us feel like we were glamping in Africa; it was very elegant. The next afternoon we saw that all the animals had gone to join the huge migration across the wide Maasai Mara. There were thousands of them: wildebeests, zebras, and various other four-legged animals.

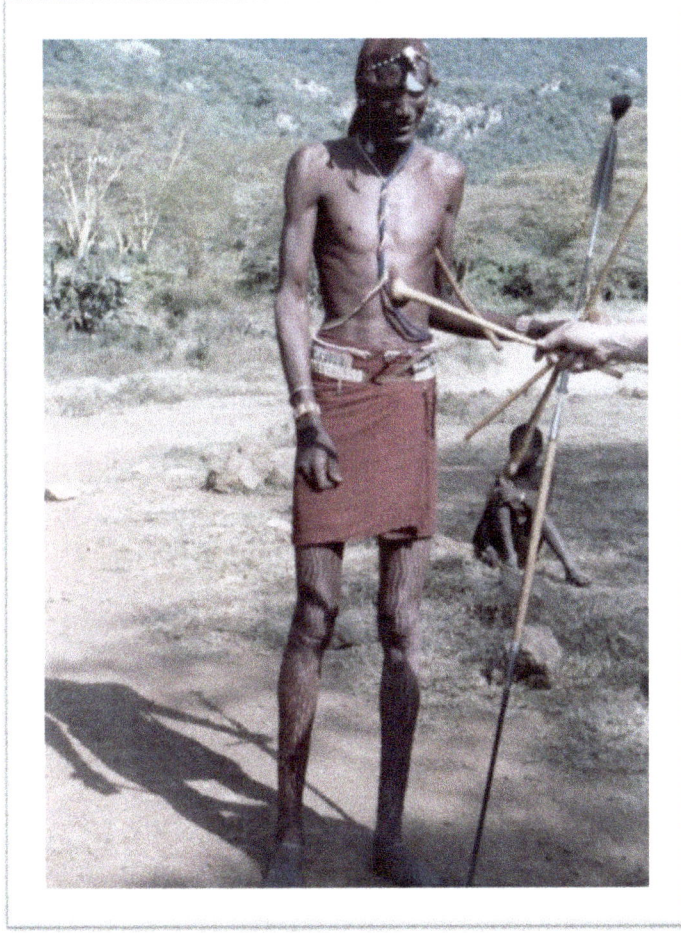

A Maasai villager.

At our next stop, Lake Nakuru Lodge, our lodgings overlooked a watering hole. We had a large deck outside our room. The animals arrived at the watering hole in a set order: first the elephants, next the rhinos, then the lions, the leopards, etc. At the end of the line were the smaller animals. The parade lasted for a long time. Amazingly, there was no fighting about the places among the animals in line. It was wonderful, and there were martinis.

An elephant herd near Mount Kilimanjaro in Amboseli National Park.

    One morning, while driving through Amboseli National Park, we observed a mother topi (a type of antelope the size of an average horse and with a single horn) watching over her baby. A short distance away, we saw the swiftest of the cats moving toward the baby topi. It moved like a shot. The mother topi was ready. She lowered her head and faced the cat. They had a furious fight. The cat went for her throat, but she drove him off. That was a high point for our entire group, watching the mother topi protect her baby. One of our group's members got the entire event on film, which we viewed that evening accompanied by more great martinis. While watching the film, the women were all rooting for the mother topi to save her baby. It was a very memorable evening.

    Our tour also took us to the Mzima Springs in Tsavo National Park. The park was home to many hippos and crocodiles. When we arrived, we headed to our cabin, which was quite nice; however, someone had left the door open, and the wall was covered with mosquitos. We didn't know who to call for help. The wall was solid with insects waiting to eat us for dinner. Gwen and I got towels and soaked them in water and killed what seemed like thousands of the critters.

Gwen and John relax at their lodge.

We then visited Mombasa Island, a coral outcrop connected to the city of Mombasa by a causeway. We were impressed by the giant tusk archway into the town and its celebration of Swahili culture. We also had tea at the Maasai Mara's Mayers Ranch, which was owned by the tribe but eventually shut down because the government thought visitors were being taken advantage of.

Kenya was a far cry from the San Francisco Zoo, and an experience I would never forget.

***

—*Zimbabwe and Botswana*—

After our tour of Kenya, we were anxious to see more animals. Of course, there were many other places of great interest in Africa, but I had read a series of novels about Botswana that compelled me to want to travel there. The nation was said to be essentially more English in character.

Victoria Falls.

We started at Victoria Falls in Zimbabwe, and I did not expect what a start that would be. Victoria Falls is one of the seven wonders of the natural world. We stayed at the Hotel Victoria Falls in the national park. We took advantage of the short time available to visit a particular portion of the falls. Just below the lip of the canyon, where the Zambezi River plummets some 355 feet, was a walkway carved into the side. We were issued raincoats, as there was a considerable amount of moisture in the air. The most impressive sight was a huge fall on the far lip that was said to be the size of Niagara Falls, yet was only a small part of the complex that makes up Victoria Falls. Returning the next morning, we found the falls to be much more extensive than we had expected. I got some remarkable pictures with my new Nikon lens.

> **From Gwen's travel diary**: *Sunny and hot, going to Victoria Falls. Very full of water, big mists, our driver has slickers and hats for everyone. The falls are similar to Iguazú Falls in Brazil, but higher. Tonight we take a gentle, two-hour cruise on the Zambezi River at sunset and see a little wildlife.*

But our ultimate goal was Botswana. I was excited to visit Botswana, because I had read some of the books in Alexander McCall Smith's *The No. 1 Ladies' Detective Agency* series, and the Botswana locale inspired me to want to travel there. While waiting for the bus, we had time to bargain for a good carving typical of the area. The landscape of Botswana was different from others we had seen in Africa. There were trees with many birds, often with bright plumage.

We arrived and were housed in a well-equipped tent that included a sack for laundry that would be returned later the same day, a wonderful service for travelers. There was a notice that the bar was open twenty-four hours. Meals were served in a covered but open area. While we were getting settled, an alarm went off. We had no idea what it meant. It turned out that a very young hippo was crashing through the tent area, obviously lost. It should be noted that even a young hippo is no small animal. Somehow workers drove him back to a nearby river. We all calmed down over dinner with drinks and some rather good wine.

Gwen and John (back row) ready to go on a safari.

  The next morning we set out on our first safari. Unlike our safaris in Kenya, we didn't see large groups of animals, but rather a broader variety, and many more birds due to more trees in the area. Midday we had an elegant picnic lunch. I used lots of film that day. Gwen particularly enjoyed the beds in our tent!

  We traveled to our next stop in a very small plane. We began to see elephants. It was wonderful to see the animals from above, and it appeared that our plane didn't bother them. Our tent accommodations were similar to the tents we had just stayed in. What was different was a nearby small community of pygmies. They were used to tourists and were eager to trade with us. We were happy to discover that we had some items to trade, but unfortunately they did not have much that interested us.

***

—Egypt—

In 1979, there was a blockbuster exhibition at San Francisco's De Young Museum, *The Treasures of Tutankhamun*, which featured the contents of the child king's tomb. Its purpose was to raise money for the museum in Cairo. The exhibition stirred our interest in Egypt. We decided to go there, and on our return, we'd stop in Chicago so I could take the Oncology Boards.

Our route to Egypt was via Rome aboard United and from there to Cairo with Japan Air. The remarkable thing was the economy seats—Gwen and I could hardly fit in them. The airport in Cairo was mayhem. No one could tell us where to go. Finally, a middle-aged man in a clean white shirt asked if he could help us. He spoke good English, so I figured, "Why not?" He quickly got our luggage and a cart. I told him we would need a taxi. He plowed through the mob and sat us in a quiet, comfortable area. He then began to tell us about a tour he could arrange. I told him we already had a tour. What we needed was a taxi to get to our hotel. He pointed to an area where taxis came. I offered him a generous tip. He wouldn't take it.

The taxi area was wild. A well-dressed young man offered to get us a taxi. I watched him get in the middle of the street and stop in front of a moving cab. I told the young man the name of the hotel, and we were on our way after he asked if he could travel with us. It turned out he was a medical student in Cairo. I had been worried that this was all some sort of scam. When we arrived at the hotel, I went to pay the cabdriver, and he said the young man had paid. I had not paid for anything since we had landed. I thanked the young man and gave him my card in case he ever got to the US. Interestingly, years later after graduating, he came to San Francisco, and I got him a short-term appointment at UCSF.

Our hotel, the Sheraton Cairo Hotel & Casino, was close to the National Museum. We had been warned to take flashlights to the museum. Although the museum had raised a good deal of money through its US tour, only a part of the museum had been upgraded. For 80 percent of our visit there, the flashlights were useful. In spite of all this, the museum was wonderful.

Wandering around the city. I found a respectable-looking store where I ordered a lightweight jacket to be picked up on our return to Cairo. More about this later.

On our first morning, we met in the lounge of our riverboat, the *Delta*, for an introductory talk by our leader, Sir Cyril Aldred. The boat was tied up on the Nile not far from our hotel. This was our first visit to the boat. It was not large and mostly wooden. It had a prominent smokestack, and the staterooms, which had screen doors, all opened to a deck that surrounded the boat. There was an upper deck with comfortable chairs. This was covered by an awning, so we could sit there in comfort and watch the action on the riverbanks. There was also a comfortable lounge with a bar and tables for meals.

Sir Cyril had been knighted by Queen Elizabeth for his work on Egypt. He spoke with a charming English accent and enunciated very well. He was of medium height and was the quintessential Englishman in appearance and manner. There was a small desk with a number of books about Egypt that Sir Cyril had written. We bought a copy of his book, *Tutankhamun's Egypt*, for $3.95. He provided us with a greatly detailed, minute-by-minute itinerary of our forthcoming trip up the Nile. Gwen added her own notes to the printed material in the margins, which was useful in reviewing where we had been and where we were going.

Gwen and I were invited to dinner by a pleasant couple we met at the break and learned that our group of about twenty-eight people would be divided into three. First was a small band of professionals, including a professor of ancient history from Oklahoma, dubbed "The Scouts." The second group, which included us, was "The Light Infantry." Sir Cyril would lead this group. The third group was "The Heavy Dragoons." This was the largest group and was to be led by the Egyptian guide. We had dinner on the boat and were told it had a large supply of bottled water and an English water filter.

Our dinner companions invited us to join them again. She said that we were the first Americans they had met who did not ask her husband, "What do you do?" We later learned that he was the curator of the Victoria and Albert Museum.

One of the step pyramids at Saqqara.

We finally got started on the sort of adventure we had expected, the cruise up the Nile. The first day had been mostly a bus tour of Cairo, a city we found had little charm or beauty. But the next day we sailed up the Nile to Saqqara, where some of the oldest pyramids stood. They had been formed in steps. The most impressive part was the colonnade that led up to the pyramids. Gwen was impressed that Sir Cyril was able to point out that texts carved in stone here were copies of those found in another place and carved in clay. Tourists who visited this spot thousands of years ago were pictured in carvings! We returned to our riverboat, where we enjoyed our first lunch on our awning-covered top deck.

  Gwen was becoming more and more fond of Sir Cyril. The time of day that appealed to Gwen the most was when Sir Cyril reviewed what we seen that day and talked about the plan for the next day, all while Gwen would be sipping her favorite vodka from the well-stocked bar.

  As we finally began our journey up the Nile, sitting in comfortable deck chairs, we could watch the action on the shore. Unfolding before us was a glimpse of life that stretched back a thousand years. For example, we could watch people lowering a long lever with a bucket on the end into the Nile and use weights to raise it back up so they could easily collect water for their animals and to irrigate their land. We could also watch animals come to the river to drink. Here we got to know our fellow passengers, who turned out to be a sophisticated group. Then there was nap time and a chance for me to grab some study time for the Oncology Boards.

> **From Gwen's travel diary**: *Everyone on board has a room on the deck with shade. 10 AM, coffee and lecture. We're skipping the afternoon part and doing only the morning trips, however, we did go on a hot excursion one afternoon to the Tombs of the Middle Kingdom. Food is better than I expected. Right after sunset is the most beautiful time: soft beige light, everything in pastel tones, white birds flying to a tree, water buffalo, and the happiest hippos in Egypt, with just their snouts above water, contented creatures with their ears wiggling.*

Each day we'd start early in the morning. After a light breakfast, we would leave the ship and explore a site for the day. We would then return for a late lunch. After a brief rest, we would usually gather on the top deck to chat and watch the riverbanks pass by.

A bas-relief in the ancient city of Abydos, west of the Nile.

On our second day on the river, we went to a new area—HERE WE GOT OUR SPURS. We got to our starting point in an old but comfortable bus. We then transferred to a truck that could travel over sandy areas. It had some fairly comfortable seating. Gwen and I were in the small "Light Infantry" group with Sir Cyril.

We made a number of stops. We were then to go back to the bus stop. As we were getting ready to head back, the truck wouldn't start. Sir Cyril told us that it would be a tough but doable walk, or we could radio for a truck to pick us up. Being close to noon, it was getting hot, so we decided we would walk. Gwen had her Japanese umbrella, whose handle I had sawed off so it would fit in her suitcase. She was a big hit. Finally, after we had been walking for a while, the backup truck finally came and picked us up.

Dayr al-Bahri, a tomb complex in the Theban Necropolis, built in the twenty-first century BCE.

I liked the wall paintings in the tombs, which often portrayed the life of the occupant. The colors were amazingly vibrant after the passage of thousands of years. They were lit mostly by sunlight directed with mirrors held by our guides. Sometimes, the more famous murals, such as those of Tut, would be lit by a light bulb. One of the depictions that changed were those of the gods. There were times it was cats that were holy, and other times crocodiles.

Our last stop was Abu Simbel; from there we were to take a plane to Cairo. The plane was a sad-looking Russian passenger plane. Shortly after takeoff, there was a steady dripping of water, most likely from the air conditioning. Our fellow passengers tried all manners of coverings. Gwen solved the problem by opening her trusty parasol. It worked! Some of the plane's decorations "ran." Thankfully, we landed safely in Cairo, to be greeted by our bus, which took us to the relative luxury of our hotel. I had excellent lamb chops for dinner accompanied by a mediocre red wine.

The next day would be marred by a bad experience. When I went to pick up the lightweight safari jacket for which I had been carefully measured and left a deposit prior to our cruise up the Nile, the manager said that he had no record of the transaction. He offered me a sleazy jacket, which I refused. I left feeling I had been taken.

As I was telling Gwen about what had happened, one of our friends in the group overheard me and asked if he could help, since he spoke the language. He took me back to the shop and threatened to report the incident to the Tourist Police. The manager immediately returned all of my deposit. (Having said he had no record of the order, he knew the exact amount of the deposit I had left off the top of his head!)

CHAPTER NINE

Southeast Asia:
Burma (Myanmar) • 1983 / Cambodia • 1996

—Burma—

For our first trip to Southeast Asia, we joined a small group traveling to Burma, now called Myanmar. While we were waiting to board our plane at the airport, Gwen met a young woman who said she would be traveling with us. She was with a group led by Sir Peter Ustinov, the acclaimed British actor and filmmaker. They were to make a film about the trip. She invited us to join their group at dinner. Gwen and I found that we got along well with the group.

The morning after our arrival in Burma, we went to a spectacular area in the middle of Yangon (formerly known as Rangoon), the capital of Burma. At the entrance to the complex, there were magnificent gold cones, and nearby many beautiful temples built by a wealthy local nobleman. By this time everyone except Gwen was calling me Sir John.

The Shwedagon Pagoda in Yangon.

> **From Gwen's travel diary**: *Our guide told us [Shwedagon Pagoda] is one of the most popular pagodas in the world. . .considered the crown of Burma. Tour took us all around in our bare feet (of course). Very beautiful and peaceful. Then over to the Scott Market [or Bogyoke Aung San Market]—large market, many stalls, not too crowded. I looked at three rings—ruby, sapphire, emerald. They were asking $220 and I made an offer but didn't buy any.*

The next day we took a short flight to a dock on the Irrawaddy River, where we boarded a beautiful boat called *The Road To Mandalay*. On the way to our cabin, we passed an elegant shop that looked like it could be in central London or Paris. Gwen and I had previously traveled in Cambodia, so we were used to wearing informal clothes. At the front of the gangplank was a sign stating that gentlemen were required to wear jackets at lunch and dinner. Alas, I didn't have a jacket. Peter Ustinov's manager took me to his room, and in his closet was a whole array of jackets for me to choose from.

> **From Gwen's travel diary**: *Our boat is floating luxury, the nicest we have ever been on. Elegant, small but posh staterooms, fancy buffet at lunch, very posh sit-down dinner. We watched the sunset, very magical. Next morning, we walked ourselves to the village where our boat was docked. Nice people, everyone smiling at us; pagodas; village life. At one place we watched them doing embroidery, at another weaving.*

The next day we visited a district with hundreds of splendid temples and stupas. Apparently, they were built by wealthy Burmese as tributes to their favorite gods. Returning to our boat just at sunset, we took our shoes off and climbed a flight of stairs to a balcony on the boat, where we sat looking at the impressive landscape lit by the setting sun. We were told not to make a sound (even camera shutters were considered too loud). IT WAS A GREAT EXPERIENCE. Fortunately, I had brought a flashlight so we could make it back down the stairs in the dark.

The reclining Buddha at Temple Yangon.

That evening Sir Peter asked Gwen and me to join him for dinner. This time I wore my best batik shirt, as did Sir Peter. The group asked us to continue with them on the tour. The next day the group was scheduled to go to a kindergarten, but we decided to go off on our own to a nearby village, which was quite charming. While walking the streets of packed, yet spotless, mud, as we stood looking at a garden in front of a home, the owner came out to invite us in. The home was built around a lovely courtyard where we were served tea and cookies. It was a very pleasant time, and despite the fact that neither group spoke each other's language, we had a lovely intercultural exchange.

We then returned to Yangon, and the next day we made our way to the center of the city, where there were more magnificent temples and stupas, and we were able to tour at our leisure. We had lunch at a very British restaurant located inside a hotel.

That evening we had a goodbye dinner with our travel group at a restaurant that was in the middle of a lake, situated at the end of a long pier. The views from the restaurant were splendid, and the vistas were framed by the restaurant's beautiful architecture. We had taken great pleasure in our day-to-day conversations with Sir Peter. In fact, we really enjoyed our time with the entire group, but sadly it was the end of that portion of our trip, so we parted company.

Gwen and I had traveled a great deal by this time, and we were surprised that Burma's beautiful architecture far surpassed that of most of the places we had visited. I didn't understand why more people didn't visit there. I think that the world was angry at the Burmese for the way their government was treating an ethnic minority of Muslims, a problem that continues to this day.

***

—Cambodia—

I had long had an interest in Cambodia. Traveling there via Hong Kong, we were surprised to find few tourists. The architecture of Phnom Penh, the capital, was more modern than we were expecting. From there, we traveled to Siem Reap to view the remarkable ruins of Angkor Wat. Our small hotel was not remarkable, but it was neat and clean. To my surprise, there was an ample supply of sealed bottled water. We learned that the one large hotel there was closed for an upgrade.

Our first evening, we had a simple chicken dinner accompanied by a drinkable wine. The next day, we arranged for a guide and were met by a Thai. We started early in the day so as to be able to return in time for the tea of the day. The massive ruins of Angkor Wat were divided into French and American sectors, with each country supporting and maintaining its area. In the American area, thick roots had grown over some of the structures. The architecture was interesting but not as colorful as that found in Burma or Thailand.

Gwen in front of the ruins of Angkor Wat.

From Gwen's travel diary: *Summer here, but not too hot. . . .Took pictures of the Silver Pagoda and the Emerald Buddha in the museum. Pizza by the pool in the shade. . . .No streetlights, stop signs, or signals.*

In the evening, we were treated to an entertaining show of dance and song. It was hard to conceive of the horrible genocide that swept through this country in the 1970s, when more than 2,000,000 people were killed at the hands of the Khmer Rouge.

CHAPTER TEN

Japan • 1975 and 1992

—1975—

When I was young, among my parents' best friends were Mel and Lillian Franklin. His business dealings were mostly with Japan. They lived close by, and their home was quite Japanese. Their garden had a bridge over a stream that was stocked with goldfish. I loved going there. So, when Gwen and I were ready to travel the world, Japan was high on our list.

I had a patient who had been married to a wealthy Japanese man who had died, and she had since remarried a German architect. Her son, a vice president at Mitsubishi, had inherited the family property in Tokyo. My patient and I had become quite friendly. When she heard I was going to Japan, she appeared in my office with a new Nikon camera, which she gave me, saying, "You must be able to take good pictures if you are going to Japan." After her generous gift, I took the course that Nikon gave and was more than ready when our trip departure date arrived.

Gwen and I planned to get to Japan a couple of days ahead of the group we were joining. Much to my surprise, we were met at the Tokyo airport by my patient, her son, and her son's daughter, bearing flowers. They got us through airport customs and to our hotel and said that they would pick us up at teatime for afternoon tea at their home, which was very modern. (My patient had shared with me that she was upset that their classic Japanese home had been torn down.)

We studied a good deal for this trip. We knew we should bring gifts. We had learned that, in the upper class, proper tea was in order, complete with sweets served on paper doilies. Apparently, paper doilies were hard to find at the time, so Gwen brought a large assortment as a gift for the wife. For the son, I brought a bottle of Johnny Walker Black Label. Gwen's gift was greeted with happy giggles, and our hostess seemed pleased.

After tea, we went to the son's club on a top floor of one of Tokyo's new buildings, where we had a drink. Then we moved to a table where the five of us sat in a row, facing two hot tables where two chefs prepared our meal. The main offering was real Kobe beef. Good California wine topped it all off. We were moved to another table for dessert.

Gwen in front of the Great Buddha statue in Tokyo.

We next toured Tokyo with our group. The city was mostly new. The main museum was surprising in having much more on display than we expected after the devastation of World War II.

Later, we were picked up by my patient and her family and taken to a restaurant for a meal featuring shabu-shabu. This very hot broth was presented in an unusual Japanese-style hot pot. This was accompanied by an assortment of raw bits of food that one dipped into the broth until cooked and then ate with the chopsticks. The next day, we rejoined our group.

Attending a sushi ritual.

We asked our new friends from dinner to be sure to plan to come and see us when they were in our area. Not long after our return home to San Francisco, they did arrange to stop by. We met them at our front door, accompanied, as usual, by our German shepherd, Tasha. They thought our home was beautiful and were very impressed. Their daughter was overjoyed with Tasha. It was rare for people to have dogs in the postwar world. Gwen and I planned an American meal that included rib roast of beef, corn on the cob, apple pie, and an excellent California wine. My best memory of that night was to see our friends' daughter hugging Tasha, who loved children.

For our first trip to Japan, Gwen and I had signed up with a group recommended by our travel agent. The plan was to visit the beautiful city of Nara and then take a short cruise on the Inland Sea. Nara has a beautiful classic temple, but Gwen was taken by a huge Buddha accompanied by a suitable companion. Then there was Daibutsu, the Great Buddha of Kamakura. The Daibutsu sits there in the open, his head looming above the pine trees and his face turned toward the peaceful waves of the ocean, typical of dreamland Nirvana. Now was the time to unveil my beautiful Nikon camera—to photograph these bronze buddhas amid their beautiful surroundings and companion sculptures.

The Katsura Imperial Villa in Kyoto

The group was taken next to a beautiful resort in Matsuyama. On the road, our leader told us that this place had three beautiful baths: one was coed, one was for women, and one was for men. No one was to wear any clothes. Gwen surprised me, saying that one of the women in our group had a beautiful body and was suggesting that the women should join the men. Again I was surprised that Gwen agreed. But as the time approached, the women in our group chose to go in the women-only bath. After our baths, we had comfortable places to rest.

> **From Gwen's travel diary**: *Our Japanese inn had mats on the floor, cold air, double kimonos, sukiyaki dinner. Good mats, bad pillows. Separate public baths are hot and steamy and look like a rock pond. Bathers sit on low benches to wash with soap and water, rinse off, then soak.*

Our next stop was Kyoto. I liked this place so much that I promised myself to return. During World War II, it was recognized as a a world treasure and thus not bombed by the US. The gardens reflected the great love of Buddha particularly and featured large areas of sand carefully manicured to radiate peace. It was difficult for me to understand that a culture that could produce such beauty could produce such a violent war machine.

> **From Gwen's travel diary**: *Today we visited the 1,200-year-old Kiyomizu-dera Temple in Kyoto, one of the most beautiful Buddhist temples in all of Japan.*

Our first trip ended with a cruise on the Inland Sea, sandwiched among Japan's main islands of Honshu, Shikoku, and Kyushu. Though it seemed like a lake, it opened onto the ocean on both ends. The scenery was peaceful. While in this region, our first major stop was the Ohara Museum of Art in Kurashiki, with its stunning collection of Western art, as well as displays of Asian and contemporary art.

—1992—

We would return to Japan several more times; it became a favorite destination for us. We loved the temples, where a big effort was made to incorporate the architecture with the nature around it. Some temples had giant sand gardens with carefully placed stones designed to free the mind and help one move to a more meditative state. These sand-and-rock gardens are called Karesansui Gardens.

In 1992, we returned to Japan again, this time renting a small, two-story home in the garden of the Hirota Guest House in Old Kyoto. These types of rentals are usually rented to Japanese, not tourists. We slept on futons on the floor. Our little house had a dining area with the recession in the ground for putting our feet.

Gwen writing travel notes at their rented accommodations in Old Kyoto.

In the morning I would go to the market and buy things for breakfast. I bought beautiful fruit from California—it was so funny to me to go all the way to Japan to buy fruit from my own state. Crazily, it looked better and tasted better than any fruit I had eaten in California. The markets also had interesting pastries, and I would bring my treasures home and prepare food for Gwen. I got to know the vendors in the market, and they were always helpful in suggesting things for me to buy.

John in front of their lodgings.

On this tour, we also enjoyed a return visit to the Ohara Museum of Art in Kurashiki, as well as a visit to a toy museum. The Japanese make wonderful toys; they were ingenious at making animated toys, even before the technology that exists today. I still have some of the toys I purchased on that trip.

Gwen and John on their 1992 trip to Japan.

One of the high points of our trip was that a daughter of a patient of mine who went to Stanford offered to help me with our stay. The first night that we moved into our rental, she rode a bicycle over to pick us up. I asked her to choose her favorite restaurant for us all to go to. I told everyone to order all their favorite things. Coincidentally, my brother was staying at a luxurious hotel in Kyoto, and when I told him about our dinner the first night, he said that our whole dinner with drinks and everything cost as much as a single dish would cost where he was staying. On the weekend, we were driven into the countryside, where we stopped at a restaurant with a beautiful stream flowing through the restaurant. Patrons scooped the noodles out of the stream. The water was hot, and the noodles were delicious.

A railroad station near us had many food stalls inside it. Each place had its own specialty. Gwen really like the Japanese-style noodles. We'd take a streetcar to the station and have dinners and lunches there. We enjoyed all the little shops too. When we left Kyoto, we went back to the Inland Sea to visit the museums again on our own. We also wanted to spend more time in the toy museum and buy things to bring home. This trip where we stayed in our little house in Old Kyoto turned out to be one of our favorite trips to Japan.

CHAPTER ELEVEN

China • 1981

We waited until 1981 to make our first major trip to China. As I have often said, my interest in the Orient dates back to my father and mother's good friends, the Franklins, whose lives and business were heavily involved with the Orient. This first visit of ours was set up by a government agency.

We ended up flying into Beijing around midnight, much to our horror. We learned that we were to be put up at a hotel about an hour outside of Beijing, where we were taken to a local hotel that had a typical Chinese hotel ambience; the hotel was surprisingly excellent. The hoteliers immediately sat us down for a meal in spite of the late hour.

The next morning after breakfast, we continued on to our hotel in Beijing, the Hilton Hotel in the Kowloon area. As we were checking in, Gwen and I noted a beautiful pair of cloisonne birds in the shop. I was told we were going to be visiting a city where such art was made. When we got to that city, it did have similar art, but unfortunately nothing nearly as nice. Near the end of our trip, we made a brief stop back at the Hilton Hotel in Beijing. The pair of birds was still there, so we purchased the set for a good sum. I can see them at this moment.

Our exploration of Beijing got underway with a visit to the impressive Summer Palace, with its beautiful architecture. Here for the first time we viewed the elegance that surrounded the royal family. As much as it was designed to impress, we didn't think it was as impressive as the Japanese architecture we had seen. We loved the Palace's tile roofs and the carved animals that represented mythological figures throughout Chinese history. We took our picture by many of the massive stone statues of guardian lions called Foo Dogs, warriors, and animals such as camels, horses, etc.

The Forbidden City in Beijing.

We stopped briefly in Tiananmen Square, where we viewed a big temple honoring Mao Tse-tung. The square, of course, would gain worldwide notoriety some eight years after our visit there as the site of the famous "Tank Man" video that we all remember as thousands of students all over China protested the government and the lack of democracy. Called the June Fourth Incident by the Chinese government today, what is known as the Tiananmen Square Massacre everywhere else marked the deaths of hundreds and possibly thousands of students; thousands more were injured. When that lone student stood in front of a tank sent to break up the protestors, halting its forward progress, he became a symbol of China's youths' protests for civil rights. The student-led movement was ultimately suppressed by the government.

We, of course, wanted to visit the Forbidden City, as it has been immortalized in so many films, most notably *The Last Emperor*. We found it to be overwhelming because of its sheer immensity. Constructed in the fifteenth century, it was dubbed a forbidden city because only the staff, employees, and government officials were allowed inside, all the way up until 1925.

On that same trip we visited the Temple of Heaven complex, one of the most beautiful collections of temples we saw in China. The architecture of the Hall of Prayer for Good Harvests is quintessentially Chinese, with its three tiers ascending from largest to smallest. The fact that the complex's various structures are still standing is amazing. From there, we visited the famous millennia-old hot springs in Chongqing (formerly referred to in the west as Chungking) and the Chongqing Hotel commune, with its many smiling school children.

Two of the highlights of our inaugural trip to China were the Great Wall and the excavated Terracotta Army in Xi'an. The Great Wall is considered one of the New Seven Wonders of the World and certainly one of the wonders in architecture. I also learned that it is the largest building project ever undertaken by humans, more than 5,000 miles long, with some of it incorporating natural barriers, such as mountains and rivers, as part of the wall. The section we saw was about an hour from our hotel. On our tour, we were very impressed with its size and the fact that we could see it winding through the hills ahead of us all the way to the horizon. The Chinese emperors, who continued its construction for centuries, wanted to protect themselves from the invaders in the North. It has stations along the wall to house troops to watch over the many parts of China. For Gwen and me, it was very impressive that such a substantial structure made of bricks and mortar could have been built before modern times. Like the pyramids of Egypt, it was hard for us to imagine how this structure could be built with such primitive equipment. The builders obviously found very creative ways to build this structure. They must have had many slave laborers, but surely these workers had to have been fairly well-treated to be up to the task.

The terracotta warriors of Xi'an.

Our second great adventure was our visit to Xi'an to view the famous Terracotta Army of soldiers. They were discovered by a farmer in his field who was digging a well in 1974, but the partial excavation didn't open to the public until 1979. We arrived in 1981, when it was still a fairly recent discovery. They hadn't excavated much of the area then, only about 200 soldiers, Now, I hear there are 8,000 soldiers on view, and much of the site still remains buried. There are eight types of soldiers, and they were made by some 720,000 artists, who all signed their names on the foot of each soldier. They started sculpting these soldiers in 246 BCE, and they finished forty years later in 206 BCE. The soldiers stand all poised and ready to go into battle for the emperor, who came to power at thirteen years of age. Qin Shi Huangdi, who proclaimed himself the first emperor of China, wanted protection in his afterlife. He must have known his country was in turmoil, because a new political group came into power after his death. For Gwen and me, it was fascinating to see the clay soldiers up close and personal. They have such real faces and expressions. The impressive thing about this was that each soldier was exactly the same size, yet the faces and hair styles where all different. The carving on each soldier was designed to reflect his position in the Chinese army. They were enclosed in huge tunnels and organized by ranks, and in addition to the soldiers, there were terracotta horses and chariots. Some of the terracotta figures were sent around the world to museums to raise money for more excavations. The authorities knew there were many more warriors to be uncovered.

A parade of monks at the Louguantai Temple.

We visited several other places of interest while we were in Xi'an: the Great Goose Pagoda, the Great Mosque, and the Bell Tower, just three of the city's many monuments. It seemed like an affluent city. Traveling southwest of the city, we stopped in a small village to see the Louguantai Temple, the ancient Taoist temple where Lao Tzu, a sixth-century-BCE contemporary of Confucius and the founder of Taoism, is said to have written the Tao Te Ching.

Another of our favorite adventures on this trip was our cruise up the Yangtze River on an old boat that dated back to the early twentieth century and resembled San Francisco's old ferries. We were a bit disappointed in the scenery, though. We found the banks of the river to be not very picturesque, as the river is a major waterway used to transport goods and services. We also thought that third-class passengers might have been cooking with fires on the lower level!

We also visited the city of Guilin, named after the forest of sweet Osmanthus trees located in the region and famous for its rice noodles. The city has also long been renowned for its karst topography. Relics found in the city's Baojian and Zengpiyan caves date back approximately 10,000 years. The landscapes surrounding the city look like many Chinese brush paintings. We were fascinated by the rounded mountains that represented thousands of years of erosion. Their fields for growing crops like rice are so vast it makes our rice fields in California look small in comparison. The city's preserved architecture made us feel like we had gone back in time. We liked this area so much we visited it again.

Also on our agenda was the storied city of Luoyang, located on the central plain of China. One of the oldest cities in China, it's considered the cradle of Chinese civilization, being the capital city of thirteen ancient dynasties and the eastern starting point of the Silk Road that linked China to the West. While there, we visited several of its main attractions, including the Longmen Grottoes, more than 2,300 caves and niches carved into the limestone cliffs lining the Yi River. The detailed carvings in the caves are considered to be a high point of Chinese stone carving and represent art from the late Northern Wei and Tang dynasties (316–907 CE).

A limestone carving of Buddha at the Longmen Grottoes in Luoyang.

Before we left on this trip, one of my patients who conducted a lot of business with China had suggested a Beijing restaurant to us, and luckily we were able to find the location. A few others in our group joined us.

We had an excellent meal there consisting of many courses of beautifully prepared Chinese food, all very fresh and elegantly presented. We really enjoyed the Peking Duck. When it came time to go back to the hotel, the streets were empty, and we spotted only one car for hire. There wasn't room for Gwen and me, so we waited for the next car, which turned out to be the same car that took us there originally. We had to wait a long time, but the meal was still worth it. On this outing, we discovered that the least expensive restaurants are found on the street level, with restaurants getting more expensive the higher the floor.

John with a sculpture of a lion in a garden in Shanghai.

    We also visited Shanghai on this first visit to China. Interestingly, I had a patient who was involved in selling heavy machinery to China, while her husband dealt mostly with Chinese art. When she heard we were going to China, she told us about what she considered to be the best shop in China. On an excursion to a lovely temple outside Shanghai, we spotted a shop adjacent to it that sounded like the one my patient had recommended. I told our tour leader that I might have found the shop, but he swore me to secrecy. He didn't want the group using up time in the shop. Gwen and I, however, were permitted a quick look-around. We bought a lovely bowl with a dish and a lid for my mother. The shop owner pointed out to me the there was a slight flaw on the underside, or else it would be museum quality. We bought another for ourselves, not quite as nice. I still have them both, having inherited the pieces from my mother. It was unbelievable that I would stumble upon the shop. Nevertheless, I kept my promise to our tour leader and never told the group about the shop.

During our government-planned tour, kindergartens were a highly favored destination. They had a certain charm, but one was enough for Gwen and me. While visiting a kindergarten in Beijing, we slipped away and went to a nearby town. As we walked down the main street, we collected a small mob who had never seen Americans. We had the temerity to go into a nice-looking shop, as Gwen decided she could use a light pair of shoes. She took one of her shoes off to show the size she wanted. The women following us paid particular attention when she opened her purse to pay. They crowded in to see what Gwen had in her purse. In another shop we saw a man making "chops," stamps that reproduce a symbol of a surname. When it came time to make mine, it needed wax or an ink pad. There was neither in the shop. A Chinese bystander seemed to understand what I wanted. I left Gwen with other customers as the man took me across a busy street to a small shop. In the back of the shop on a shelf was a proper ink pad. After I purchased a couple of these, the helpful man guided me back to Gwen, who by this time was worried. I offered the man some money, which he refused. I think he may have been insulted. I had a lot to learn. Of course I thanked this kind man.

When we rejoined our group, the leader was not too happy with us. In our many travels, we had learned to avoid groups, but at that time, we had no choice as groups were mandatory in China.

Yet somehow Gwen and I got away again. We took a walk along a river and noticed a tall cliff on the opposite side. Carved into that cliff was a colossal Buddha supported by two huge gods. I couldn't find mention of this impressive site in any of our guidebooks.

One of the best days during our first trip to China involved the then-acting governor of Hong Kong. Our good friend Betty Ackerman had dialed him earlier. He invited Gwen and me to a luncheon at the local racetrack in Hong Kong. There was a group of about ten of us, which included the Chief Justice of the Supreme Court of Hong Kong and his wife. His wife, coincidentally, ended up being a patient of mine back in San Francisco. Gwen had the winning ticket in one of the races, which she gave to the governor.

There is another interesting Hong Kong–related anecdote. Before our trip, one of the doctors at UCSF referred a woman visiting from Hong Kong to me for an operation. All went well. When she heard that I was to be in Hong Kong, she and her husband insisted that I save them a day. When I told the referring doctor, she said, "You must accept. You think that you know rich people, but you don't know really until you know rich people from Hong Kong." So, Gwen and I accepted. On the day I had saved for them, we were picked up by a seven-passenger Mercedes for a cruise around the Hong Kong harbor. Already on board the vessel were the aforementioned patient, her husband, and the grandfather. As we circled the island of Hong Kong, we stopped on the mainland side at a small village, where we had a snack. On the bay side, we stopped at a small bayside restaurant. The restaurant had a huge fish tank; the grandfather escorted me over to it to help me pick out the fish for our dinner. The meal was excellent. I got to know the family well. They subsequently moved to Canada, taking their clothing business with them, after Great Britain transferred its sovereignty over Hong Kong back to the People's Republic of China in 1997—a good move for the family.

We never tired of Hong Kong. We would visit it or pass through it again and again over the years. The ferry ride to Kowloon was one of the of the best buys in China (usually less than ten cents).

The busy harbor in Hong Kong.

In later years, we enjoyed visiting Shanghai. We particularly liked the French Quarter, which was reminiscent of a French suburb. The hotel we loved to stay at was the Sheraton Shanghai Waigaoqiao, which had a splendid cocktail hour, with free alcoholic drinks and eleven kinds of delicious small servings—all complimentary to hotel guests. We found that it could be enough for dinner, saving us from having to run out and find places to eat.

Shanghai's museums are among some of the world's best. We found ways to beat the long lines. We would wait for a large group of Americans and join them—IT WORKED! We would spend hours at these museums, and no one bothered us. One night in Shanghai we went to a motorcycle show. The motorcycle riders were in a big, round cage. They would ride faster and faster, and the centrifugal force would keep them upright and sticking to the walls.

City lights in Shanghai, 1992.

In 1992, during one of our later trips to China, Gwen wanted to go to Suzhou outside of Shanghai to visit its famous gardens. We took the train to the city, and the cab driver we got at the train station insisted on taking us to a place for lunch. It was good, but then the driver wouldn't take us to the garden that Gwen wanted to see (Suzhou has five classic gardens). We finally found a cab with a driver who understood us, and we got to the right garden. That garden and others we visited were quite beautiful, but we found them to be less delicate than those in Japan. We got a cab to the train station with our fourth-class tickets in hand, but the ticket taker would not take them. The train was about to leave for Shanghai, but he told us to wait. He returned to take us to seats in a good section of the train that was reserved for newspapermen. The man who helped us refused a tip. We returned to Shanghai a couple of years later, much wiser about riding the rails.

We have been to China more often than to any other Asian country. We returned a number of times, each visit always bringing something new. We felt safe there. We were never cheated or robbed. We were surprised at the courteousness, friendliness, and interest we encountered. The feeling I recall about China is that one sees old cities that have preserved most of their original charm and architecture, in contrast to the modern cities like Shanghai and Hong Kong. The modern cities are much more modern than most modern cities. The intersections have walkways along and over the streets, so that pedestrians can walk many places. The roads we traveled on were mostly better and more spacious than those in the US and designed to keep the millions of Chinese moving through the country. However, they seemed to have fewer exits than the freeways in America.

CHAPTER TWELVE

South America • 1994

In our first years of traveling, we started with Europe, mainly because our family members had preceded us there. But at one point, I thought we should branch out and visit South America. I decided we should travel from north to south to explore the continent. Embarking on our South American adventure, we landed in Lima, Peru, and although Gwen liked the hotel there, the staff in the hotel didn't want us to go out alone without an escort because of the danger of thieves, etc., so we didn't see a lot of Lima. From there, we took a plane to Cusco in the Andes Mountains, where we would begin our trek to legendary Machu Picchu. After we arrived at our hotel, when we went to have our usual martini that evening, we were offered coca leaves to chew instead. When in Rome . . . ! It actually didn't taste bad, kind of like grass. Could this be the substance that gave birth to Coca-Cola, we wondered? Nonetheless, Gwen really missed her before-dinner martini.

Children in Cusco with their llamas.

The next day we took the train to Machu Picchu, not a long trip, and checked into a hotel in one of the three towns nestled beneath the magnificent ruins. Machu

Picchu, a fifteenth-century citadel strategically perched on a mountaintop, is a dramatic remnant of the Incan civilization. It's easy to see the whole city from the front gate. We joined a tour group; they told us what they knew about the city. It was obviously a well-organized society, with provisions for farm animals such as sheep and goats. It's so well-maintained today it looks as if you could live there now. It was occupied for only a century and then abandoned, known only to a few local farmers until an American explorer and academician, Hiram Bingham, stumbled upon the ruins in 1911.

John in front of the ruins of Machu Picchu, elevation 7,972 feet.

After a pleasant dinner at our hotel, we walked back over to the "Lost City of the Incas." It was so peaceful at night, and there were no tourists. In the peace and quiet, we were able to fantasize about all the people who used to live there. The site was slightly elevated on both sides, the structures consisting of small homes and buildings that had stood the test of time.

Our next stop was Manaus in Brazil, located in the very heart of the Amazon rainforest, where we stayed in a small hotel. As we enjoyed a nice dinner, a roaring fire in the courtyard kept away the mosquitos! The fire, along with a troubadour who was playing delightful Spanish music on his guitar, and the moonlight, made for a very romantic, dream setting. Although Gwen suffered some intestinal problems that night, she made a speedy recovery. In fact, the next day we went fishing and caught a few small unimpressive fish that the hotel chef cooked for us, after which we visited a town downriver that had a beautiful church.

From the Amazon basin, we headed to Brasilia, the new capital of Brazil. Though it was the capital, it was surprising how little activity there was. The city is very unusual, laid out in the shape of a bird. The modern architecture was the work of the famous urban planner, Lúcio Costa, who helped design the city, built from barren land in the high desert of Brazil in just five years. It was officially completed in 1960. The famous artist Oscar Niemeyer also contributed many ideas to the city, and the avant-garde landscape was designed by Roberto Marx. The city was originally imagined in 1789, when the Brazilian revolutionary Joaquim Jose da Silva Xavier suggested they move the capital of Brazil from Rio de Janeiro to the middle of the country. No one actually acted on this idea until 1956. Niemeyer went on to design the iconic Cathedral of Brasilia, with its curved architecture and beautiful stained-glass ceiling, situated in its prominent place in the middle of the city's government plaza.

An aerial view of Rio de Janeiro.

Finding that there really wasn't much to see in Brasilia, we decided to move on to our next stop, Rio de Janeiro, taking a train there and staying in the city's Ipanema neighborhood. We were at a hotel right across the street from the beach. We were warned not to take anything to the beach because it would be stolen, but we took our chances with a beach visit so we could swim in the warm water. Gwen left her fancy jewelry behind, wearing pieces made of wood or inexpensive stones. She always looked so elegant no matter where we traveled. The second day we had intended to take the tram to the top of Sugarloaf Mountain and also visit the mammoth art deco Christ the Redeemer statue, sitting at the top of Mount Corcovado above the city. The statue was dedicated in 1931 and chosen as one of the New Seven Wonders of the World in 2007. However, the stories we were hearing about thieves and crime made us feel uncomfortable, so we decided to skip the tram ride, go directly to the Christ statue, and move on. Although the district surrounding our hotel with its many small boutiques looked attractive, the doorman discouraged us from walking around the neighborhood too much.

John and Gwen in front of the Copacabana Palace hotel.

We did, however, visit the famous jewelry store in Rio called H. Stern. The jewelry was expensive, but the loose stones were reasonable. We bought stones for a ring, bracelet, and necklace, and later had them set in New York at a jewelry store with a good reputation. Gwen wore the ring for many years—up to, in fact, the day she left this world.

We next headed to Paraty, situated on Brazil's Costa Verde between Rio de Janeiro and São Paulo. The city was very interesting to Gwen and me, because it was so unlike anything else we had seen in Brazil. It was a small city with no vehicles, so when we arrived, someone from our hotel came to meet us on foot when we arrived in town. From there, we walked to the hotel as porters carried our luggage for us. Paraty has a beautiful Portuguese colonial city center, as well as great access to the ocean. After settling in at our hotel, we went with a group by sailboat to a local spot and brought our lunch with us to eat there. We didn't know ahead of time that we would be able to swim, but when others in our group went swimming in the ocean, it looked so attractive I decided to go swimming in my underwear while Gwen watched our things. (I couldn't convince her to go swimming in her underwear!) I loved the bath-like water, and it turned out to be one of the best ocean-swimming experiences I've ever had.

Gwen and John at Iguazú Falls.

From Paraty, we flew back to Rio and caught a flight to the great Iguazú Falls. We stayed at a beautiful hotel right near the falls, surrounded by beautiful scenery. Iguazú Falls, straddling the border of Argentina and Brazil, is the largest waterfall complex in the world. We were certain that these were the most beautiful falls we had ever seen. I elected to fly over the falls in a helicopter, but Gwen, leery about boarding a rather rickety whirlybird, opted out and would meet me later. I used a whole roll of film on that trip. Alternatively, Gwen found a place where one could take an elevator down to the lower level of the falls. We both had great adventures to share when we met up later. The falls reminded us of Victoria Falls in Africa; Niagara Falls is small in comparison. We were amazed by how much land these falls covered.

From there we flew to Buenos Aires, the capital of Argentina. We stayed at one of the most beautiful hotels we have ever been in, the Alvear Palace Hotel. The breakfast buffet there was incredible; they had a whole table full of just berries. While in Buenos Aires, we visited the graveyard where Eva Peron's tomb is. The cemetery, where many other famous people are buried, is a major tourist stop. For us, the most memorable food in Argentina was at a *churrascaria* restaurant where *churrasqueiras* cook *churrasco*-style, seasoning the meat with salt and cooking it over hot coals and wood, turning it until it's cooked just right. Then they serve it at your tableside and cut off pieces you want to try until you are full. One can order any kind of meat one would like. Our meal was delicious. The Portuguese word *churrasco* translates roughly in English to "barbecue."

We also took a trip outside the city to watch the famous Argentinian gauchos (or cowboys) demonstrate their equestrian skills, performing all manner of challenging acrobatics on horseback.

From Buenos Aires, we drove through a pass called the Paso Pehuenche amid some beautiful mountains between Argentina and Chile. We were captivated by the Chilean town of Puerto Varas, with its colonial homes built by German immigrants in the 1900s. A helpful native steered us to a seafood place that was so good we went back a second time. We also visited the town of Frutillar on Llanquihue Lake, with its black sand beaches and German colonial-style architecture. Just passing through Santiago, Chile's capital, we continued on to the seaside town of Vin del Mar (or Vineyard of the Sea), which we loved for its gardens, beaches, and museums.

We then moved on to Valparaiso on the west coast of Chili, where we visited the home of Chile's most famous poet, Pablo Neruda. His home, on a hill looking out over the ocean, reminded us of similar neighborhoods in San Francisco.

CHAPTER THIRTEEN

New York City • 1958–2016

Although I had been to Manhattan with my mother and father many times, with either one or both of them, I was anxious to return there, as I had a lot of fond memories of those trips to "the Big Apple." The aforementioned travel editor at the *San Francisco Chronicle*, Stanton Delaplane, always had good suggestions for visiting New York City, so I got many of my Manhattan travel ideas from him. (His biggest claim to fame was introducing Irish coffee to America by way of San Francisco's Buena Vista Café.) When Gwen and I took our first trip to Europe together in 1958, on our return trip we made arrangements to stop in New York City for a week to rest up before returning San Francisco. We had left our children with Gwen's mother and our trusted housekeeper, so we had the luxury of extending our journey.

> **From Gwen's travel diary**: *Our flight from London to New York lasted forever. The dawn would never come; they kept resetting the clock. Stopped in Goose Bay [Newfoundland]; to refuel because of strong headwinds—snow on the ground. I figure our flight took 17 hours. That adds up to SOME flying! Funny to hear everyone speaking "American" again.*

I remember that on our first night in New York, Gwen and I had tickets to a top Broadway show, and I didn't want to miss it, because we had been able to get good seats. During our stay, we took in all the usual tourist attractions and also paid a visit to the 21 Club at 21 West 52nd Street, with its iconic jockey statues lining the front of the club.

From Gwen's travel diary: *After the show we went to "21" for a supper of broiled lobster and broccoli with hollandaise. Sitting right next to us was the cast of the just-premiered movie,* Roots of Heaven, *Trevor Howard, Errol Flynn, Juliette Gréco, and Darryl F. Zanuck. New York is most exciting.*

This was the first of many trips we took together to New York City over the course of the next half century, and Broadway shows and visits to the 21 Club would become staples of our visits there. Gwen and I got into the habit of going to "21" on our anniversary, trying to make it there every year. (Luckily, the weather in New York is relatively good in June.) We had a favorite table at the "21" bar, where they had toys and airplanes hanging from the ceiling. Whenever I called to make a reservation and gave my last name, they would always ask us if we wanted our regular table. One year they gifted us with a very fine bottle of wine, a Quintessa 2010, for our anniversary. On more than one occasion, while walking from our hotel to the club, people would say to us, "You are such a cute couple," or variations thereof. On our fiftieth wedding anniversary, we walked past a large group of young people, and one couple in the group asked us where we were going. When we told them, these kids sang to us and made a big deal out of our anniversary by escorting us to the club. We enjoyed that very much.

On our first trip to Europe, we met a couple from St. Louis, Missouri, the Aaronsons, and we became lifelong friends. Up until World War II, Adam Aaronson was in the camera business, but after the war he opened banking institutions all along the Mississippi Valley. He and his wife donated a sculpture garden to the city of St. Louis. The couple had an apartment at the elegant 23 Beekman Place in Manhattan, and they offered to let us stay in their apartment whenever we visited New York, even for as long as a month every summer if we wanted. The famous composer Irving Berlin lived in that same apartment complex. In fact, Gwen and I were staying there in May 1988 when Berlin was sung to on his 100th birthday by admirers a year before he died. A favorite cousin of mine, John Kapstein, also had an apartment at Beekman Place, even though after World War II he lived mostly in Paris. During the war, he flew in the unit that inspired the book *Catch 22*. Flying more than the allotted twenty missions, he was able to bring his crew home safely every time. Gwen and I loved hanging out with him and would do so any chance we got.

Gwen in front of Le Cirque restaurant in Manhattan.

Dining out at restaurants in New York was important to Gwen and me because we had so many favorites, going to them before the theater or when meeting friends. Occasionally, when visiting New York, we would dine with John Colby, the publisher of my second and third books, *A Combat Medic Comes Home* and *San Francisco Heroes I Have Known*, and the publisher of this book.

The New York skyline with the Twin Towers, 1986.

At one point, the Aaronsons introduced us to Danny Meyer, the son of some friends of theirs in St. Louis. He was the owner of a top-flight New York restaurant called the Union Square Cafe. We had already planned to go there, because we'd heard that he was one of the best restaurateurs in New York. Having been personally introduced to him, we in turn were treated especially well whenever we dined there. In addition to the Union Square Cafe, Meyer owned several other restaurants in New York that always got top ratings, and we were always greeted wonderfully when we went to any one of them. The most recent of his restaurants was in the new Museum of Modern Art, where the wait staff treated Gwen and me to lots of fun, delicious dishes to taste. It was one of our favorite restaurants—an elegant place with small, beautifully presented dishes.

We also regularly patronized the restaurant in the French consulate down the street from the Museum of Modern Art. On one of my more recent visits there, I was wearing my French Legion of Honor ribbon, which they immediately recognized. They were extra-delighted to have us as diners. The same thing happened when we went to the very French, very classic Chevalier Restaurant in the small yet elegant Baccarat Hotel at 20 West 53rd Street, where we were treated like honored guests. The very first time we went there, the maître d' called all the employees together to meet me because of the French Legion of Honor ribbon on my jacket. Everyone was quite impressed by the honor bestowed upon me. Gwen really enjoyed having the opportunity to speak French with the staff, who were all fluent in the language.

Balthazar in SoHo was another favorite New York eatery that we visited frequently. It was so much like the brasseries found on the grand boulevards of Paris. It was nostalgic for us, because we absolutely loved Paris, especially Gwen. She always said it was her favorite city.

Our "favorites" list grew with each visit! We also liked two restaurants that were great places to dine before the theater: the db bistro moderne at 55 West 44th Street (fast service) and Frankie & Johnnie's Steakhouse (where we would share a steak). We loved the Four Seasons Restaurant, with its large Picasso painting at the entrance. We always requested a table that looked out over a large pool. The restaurant was pretty expensive, but we thought it was worth it.

One restaurant we always looked forward to dining at when we arrived in the city was famous for its steaks and lobsters. One of us would order a steak, the other a lobster, and then we'd divide and share them.

When not staying at the Aaronsons' apartment, we would book our favorite room at the Sheraton New York Times Square Hotel, with its great views of Central Park and the New York skyline. Two of our favorite restaurants within walking distance from that hotel were Marea, a fun French restaurant, and Molyvos, a lovely Greek lunch spot located at 871 Seventh Avenue. We would often meet my cousin John there.

Finally, there was the legendary Plaza Hotel on West 59th Street across from Central Park. We would board the elevator in its elegant lobby and ride it down to the basement, which had assorted specialty shops and food courts, where we would fill up on pizza, hot dogs, or hamburgers.

Our friends—the Aaronsons, who had a large gallery in St. Louis filled with contemporary art, and the Herrringers, from Piedmont, California, who were art collectors as well—would encourage Gwen and me to see the best of the contemporary artists whenever we were heading to New York. I had studied to be a docent at San Francisco's Museum of Modern Art, and in the process, I had learned a lot about modern art. Gwen had studied art while at Stanford and was interested in more classical contemporary artists such as Matisse, Picasso, etc., whereas Mary Ellen Herringer and the Aaronsons were more interested in the leading cutting-edge artists of the current day. Gwen and I spent a good deal of time in the galleries our friends had recommended and even occasionally bought a painting for our own collection, usually after consulting with our collector friends.

Gwen and I took advantage of our trips to New York to shop for clothes for ourselves. Back at home, we always had so many other things to do: children; neighborhood organizations; and tree planting, especially on the then treeless Jackson Street, which now has beautiful trees lining the street. (Gwen developed a campaign to get the overhead telephone and electric wires moved underground. It was a long battle, but it made the entire neighborhood much more attractive and also improved real estate values in the area.)

During one of our earliest trips to New York, my cousin John introduced me to a tailor who also worked for the Lord & Taylor department store on Fifth Avenue. On every trip to New York, I visited that tailor and had something made, sometimes a suit and other times a sport jacket. I just ordered whatever the tailor recommended, because I had confidence that he committed to high quality and knew what my particular tastes were. When he retired, he referred me to someone who wasn't as good as he was, so I began buying my clothes mostly from Brooks Brothers in New York and San Francisco.

Two lovely ladies: Gwen Kerner and the Statue of Liberty.

Gwen and I loved to walk along Madison Avenue because of all its wonderful small shops, which we preferred over the big department stores. Gwen especially loved the elegant, semi-dressy clothes she would buy at these shops, delighted that many of them carried her exact size. Occasionally she bought elegant outfits for dressy affairs. Henri Bendel was her favorite place for hats and sweaters. The store's famous song went, "You're a Bendel bonnet, a Shakespeare sonnet."

One day while we were riding a bus, she saw a dress in a window. We got off the bus, and she walked back to buy the dress. When she saw something she liked, she knew right away. She had impeccable taste. She also loved shopping in the Metropolitan Museum gift shop, which always had unique items for sale.

There was a Brooks Brothers store near our hotel where I went regularly to buy clothing staples and shirts. If I liked a shirt, I often would buy one and then take it with me on our next trip to Hong Kong, where they could duplicate the shirt for half the price.

One of our earliest trips to New York was in 1952 when Gwen and I went there so that I could take the specialty board examination for OB-GYN. A doctor had to have been in practice for two years minimum, and the exam took two days. They gave us very difficult slides to read, and for the gross pathology, they presented a uterus that was turned inside out, and we had to identify all the pertinent info about that sample. They also gave us several oral examinations. At the end of the first day, we were told when to return and to whom we should report. When it was my turn to find out, the secretary said, "You don't have to come back." The thought flashed before me that maybe I'd failed, but she said, "No, Dr. Kerner, you passed after one day instead of two." I was so pleased that I didn't have to go back the next day. So, I floated back to the St. Regis Hotel, where we were staying, and met Gwen at the hotel's famous King Cole Bar for dinner and drinks. A cousin of mine, who was a buyer for Saks Fifth Avenue, had managed to obtain for us hard-to-get tickets for a new show that had just opened that week—*Guys and Dolls*! Not only did we have tickets to the show, but we also had good seats. AND I didn't have to worry about getting up early the next morning to go back to the exam. This was one of the best days of my life. It was a perfect day, in New York City with my best friend, and the knowledge that I had done my best on a test.

***

It would not be fitting to exclude this one last anecdote about visiting New York, even though this particular visit of mine predates my meeting Gwen and is quite a few years after my childhood visits to Manhattan with my mom or dad. It was May 1944. Following my being drafted in December 1943, being deployed to Pennsylvania and then to Colorado, and given a one-week leave in San Francisco, I crossed the US by train with my friend Dave Roth to a military camp in New Jersey. After a couple of weeks there, we were suddenly told to pack, not yet knowing that we would be part of the invasion in France. There was a lottery for a one-night leave in New York City, and Dave and I won! We had been given the night off, but with the threat that if we weren't back in time the next morning, the punishment would be severe. So, we headed into New York in uniform, where we treated ourselves to a fancy dinner at the Fontainebleau, starting with martinis and pâté and dining on onion soup, steak, and camembert. Just as we were finishing, a friend from San Francisco walked in, and as we chatted, how Dave and I envied his cushy Army assignment in New York, ourselves on the brink of heading into the thick of things.

We next headed to the musical *Carmen Jones*, for which we had been given tickets. It was the story of opera composer Georges Bizet's *Carmen*, with an all-Black cast. We loved the sets, done up in vivid colors, and wondered how long it would be before we would see the likes of such a spectacle again. We then went to a well-known nightclub, the Café Society Uptown, where the famous singer Hazel Scott and comedian Jimmy Savoy were on the bill. Part of Savoy's act included him singing "River, Stay Away from My Door," during which he literally got down on the floor. Also featured was Larry Adler, who played the harmonica very well. We stopped by a couple of smaller clubs before ending our club crawl at the Copacabana, where the star that night was Jimmy Durante. What a night. There I was with my best friend sitting at a front row table being given drinks on the house. The show inspired my friend to imitate Jimmy Durante—throughout the rest of the war!

When the show ended around 2 a.m., we still had a little time left, so we hailed a cab. The cabbie suggested we go to Louie the Waiter's. The staff let us in, and the owner came over and suggested we try the lox, bagels, and cream cheese. Shockingly, this West Coast–raised Jewish medical draftee didn't know what lox were! I had never been exposed to them in the Bay Area. The waiter brought in a big platter filled with some six bagels and lox with all the fixings. We hadn't eaten much that day, although we had had many drinks, so we were hungry and ate every bit of it. When we finished, we checked out another couple of clubs and wandered down Fifth Avenue before heading back to base, getting there about an hour ahead of our curfew of 6 a.m., thus avoiding that "severe punishment." Reflecting on the night we had just experienced, we couldn't help but ponder the possibility that we might never return.

The next day was a sharp and jarring contrast. We sailed from New York Harbor on a commandeered German passenger ship amidst a giant convoy. The ships with combat soldiers were in the middle of the convoy, and the bigger ships were on the outside. So crowded were we that half of us would play cards while the other half slept. I was able to earn some cash winning at hearts and bridge, but there wasn't really anywhere to buy anything. Although we were attacked by German submarines, we finally made it to Liverpool, England. It took a long time to get there, and New York was long distant. However, the memories of our splendid night in Manhattan would, every now and then, flash before me in the coming months, as I slogged through a brutal, surreal world that seemed a universe away from New York.

CHAPTER FOURTEEN

Return to the WWII Battlefields • 2003

Shortly after my first book, *Combat Medic: World War II*, was published in 2002, I was sent a copy of the San Francisco Police Department newspaper by the mother of a police lieutenant who had attended one of my book readings. In the paper was an ad for a tour of the battlefields of the Second World War in Europe. The trip was to follow the course of the 35th Infantry Division—my division!—during World War II, starting in Normandy, with visits to the landing beaches and local museums, then continuing on to Bastogne, across the Rhine to Koblenz, then down the Rhine, and ending in Berchtesgaden and Salzburg in Austria. I contacted the travel agent who had organized the tour, telling her about my book and my war experiences and expressing my interest in learning more about the trip. Given my personal, firsthand connection to the tour's destinations, the agent told us that her husband was so adamant about our coming she would offer us a substantial discount for what was already an affordable tour.

The prospect of revisiting the beaches and towns of Normandy appealed greatly to me, since it had been some fifty-eight years since my division and I had landed on Omaha Beach shortly after D-Day. And Gwen was equally enthusiastic, as the tour was to start in Paris, her favorite city. We would plan to arrive a few days early to have some additional time in the City of Light.

Our tour of the WWII battlefields of Europe started on May 14, 2003, in Paris. Our group of eight had shrunk considerably from the thirty who had originally signed on, due to several factors: the outbreak of the US war with Iraq, the weakened US economy, and the SARS outbreak. The smaller group, however, made it possible for us to travel by van rather than by bus. Our fellow travel companions were policemen and their wives, all of whom were quite a bit younger than Gwen and I. I discovered that all of them but one had read my book, *Combat Medic*! Throughout our trip, they would bend over backwards helping Gwen and me and would ask me questions constantly, which I was more than happy to answer.

After spending a short time touring Paris, our group headed to Normandy, driving in our van to the town of Creully sur Seulles, twelve miles outside of Caen. The town was just nine miles from Bayeux (of the famous tapestry) and a little more than twenty miles from Omaha Beach.

When we signed up for this tour, it was important to me that I took Gwen, as much as possible, along the exact route my division followed during the course of the war. Driving through the Norman countryside, I was reminded about how, prior to D-Day, no one in command told us soldiers about the hedgerows that cover most of Normandy and divide the landscape into small farms. At the time of the war, the hedgerows were so dense even Allied tanks had a hard time breaking through them. The Germans, on the other hand, knew the region well and were able to use the hedgerows to their advantage, attacking Allied troops with mortar shells that traveled easily over the hedgerows. I was also able to use the hedgerows to *my* advantage, using areas with heavy hedgerows to set up my aid stations in natural protected areas to treat the wounded. On this visit, we found a book in a bookstore that was all about the hedgerows, complete with hand-drawn illustrations showing all the ingenious ways the Germans used them in their battles with the French. We bought several copies of the book.

Our centuries-old hotel in Creully sur Seulles, the Hostellerie Saint Martin, had just twelve rooms, perfect for our group. Our spacious room was reached by a spiral staircase. We dined that first night in Normandy at the small but elegant hotel dining room, getting to know each other over an excellent meal of local seafood and wine.

Effigy of the US paratrooper who parachuted into the town of Sainte-Mère-Église during the Normandy invasion and ended up hanging from the roof of the town's church.

During our dessert course, a woman named Andrée Chan came over and introduced herself to our group. She was the vice president of the 35th "Santa Fe" Division in Normandy and was wearing a pin that bore the division's insignia. The group was formed to honor my division for liberating a number of Normandy towns, including the town of Giéville, of which the president of the group, Guy Latour, was the mayor. After showing us some of her collection of World War II memorabilia, Chan invited me and the rest of the group to have lunch with her two days hence.

For the next two days, our group toured the landing beaches and museums along the Normandy coast. Everywhere we went, I was greeted graciously, since word had gotten out that I had served in combat in Normandy. Museum directors presented me with diplomas, medals, and free admission. I had brought my dress uniform with me on the trip and wore it several times, along with my medals.

John and Gwen in the colonnade at the Normandy American Cemetery in Colleville-sur-Mer.

On the morning of our luncheon with Chan and her organization, after visiting Omaha Beach, we headed to the magnificently designed American Cemetery. At one end is a monument to the various units that participated in the invasion, with walls showing the progress of the Allied Forces. At the far end of the graveyard, past row after row of crosses and Stars of David, is the chapel.

I found myself fighting back tears as I thought of the many fine men we had lost in that invasion. By the time our tour of the landing beaches and cemetery ended, we were at the far end of the beach at Pointe du Hoc, where our group was met by a small delegation from our lunch hosts.

They escorted us to the locale of the luncheon, Le Motel du Bocage, a small hotel in Giéville owned by Mayor Latour. Outside of the hotel, we were met by a larger group of members, all wearing the insignia of the 35th Division.

John in front of the Signal Monument on Omaha Beach, Normandy.

From Gwen's travel diary: *Saturday, sunny, cloudy, nice. Today is John's day of honor. He wore his military uniform everywhere we went. He got lots of special attention: certificates, gifts, questions. We watched a movie about the British landing and how they built a false harbor. At the lavish lunch,* *the tables were decorated with flags and we dined on melon, white fish, boiled potatoes, vegetables, tarte aux framboise, wine, and champagne.*

John at the luncheon honoring him at the Motel du Bocage in Giéville.

There was much talk about the fact that I was hoping to find the baby girl I had delivered during the Battle of Mortain in June 1944. The mother had been brought to my aid station carried on a ladder covered by a quilt. It was fortunate that her companions had sought me out, as the baby presented as a footling breech. It is almost certain that I was the only person in a wide radius that night who could have successfully performed such a difficult birth. It was this story, which had appeared in the local papers prior to our arrival, that had alerted our hosts to our visit. One couple had come to the luncheon from the city of Nancy, some 300 miles away.

Our lunch, held in a lovely, flower-bedecked setting at a banquet table set for twenty-four people, began with a first course of melon containing a red liqueur in a lovely tulip-shaped glass, champagne, and a welcoming speech. At that juncture, having been made an honorary member of their organization, I was called upon to speak. The generosity of the occasion, combined with the morning visit to the American Cemetery, was almost more than I could bear. I am usually at ease talking in public, but on this occasion, I found myself fighting back tears. About all I could manage was a thank you. The lunch proceeded with a variety of Normandy specialties, red and white wines, and after dessert, more speeches and more gifts. People who had read my book knew how much I treasured Calvados during the invasion, so I was given a lovely bottle of the signature brandy that hails from the department of Calvados in northern France. I was also presented with a cap bearing the division insignia, a medal honoring my division, and a container of sand from Omaha Beach. At the lunch, there was a display table with information about the 35th, as well as clippings about me from the newspaper, *Ouest-France*. In addition, after the luncheon, we were taken to a small museum that Mayor Latour had filled with all sorts of equipment and other memorabilia connected with the 35th. From there, we went to the Chapel of La Madeleine, a small church that had once been part of a leper home. The church had been converted to a tribute to the division, displaying flags, other memorabilia, and plaques in honor of those who had died.

After what had been a most memorable day, we headed back to our hotel. That evening, two reporters came to the hotel to have dinner with Gwen and me. Besides interviewing me, they took pictures of me that were then used in two long articles in *Ouest-France* about my quest to find "the baby." As a result of those articles, I received many emails in which people expressed their thanks to our division, but also offered to help me in my search for the infant I had delivered in the heat of battle. Unfortunately, I was never able to find the baby, who would by then have been fifty-nine years old. I will never know if the infant survived those turbulent early days of the invasion and was out there somewhere living out a long and happy life.

Gwen and John at the luncheon hosted by the local 35th "Santa Fe" Division.

     This return trip to Normandy marked the first time I had gotten recognition for what I had gone through during World War II. Throughout our trip, local policemen would direct traffic to help our group get to our destinations easily and quickly. We felt like we had our own personal escort the entire time. The personal attention I received illustrated how much the citizens of the region still appreciated the contributions American soldiers made to the war effort.

     The day before the invasion in June of 1944, as we awaited our deployment in England, we were allowed one last letter. I wrote to my mother and told her that I didn't know what was going to happen, but that I felt like I was where I was supposed to be. We were just starting to hear about the concentration camps, so I did feel justified about attacking the Germans. Until word of the concentration camps got out, many Americans were against our participation in the war. Once in the thick of things in Normandy, as mentioned in the chapter on Berlin, we were so close to the Germans that we could hear them speaking. I could sometimes make out what they were saying, as I understood German, and I was doubly worried about being captured, since I was Jewish. All that said, when faced with wounded German soldiers, we did what was necessary to treat them. I remember one group of aid men being upset that we were giving good American plasma to the enemy. However, the Geneva Convention stated that any wounded soldiers should be treated, no matter what side they were on. Yet, most of the Germans we encountered during the course of the war never mentioned giving any care to American soldiers; in fact, during the Battle of the Bulge, the Germans captured a group of American soldiers and instead of keeping them as prisoners as dictated by the Geneva Convention, they killed the soldiers instead.

In the early days of the invasion, I found a civilian radio, and we figured out we could run it on the batteries we used for mine sweepers. With this radio I could pick up the excellent daily news broadcasts by the BBC. I would then type up a news report daily on an inherited typewriter and post my *Kapy's News* on a tree for everyone to read. (My last name then was Kapstein.)

Leaving the accolades and memories of Normandy behind us, our tour group continued on to the eastern part of France, following Patton's route with the 35th Division. Arriving in Nancy, I showed our group around, and we got to meet with a family I knew there from the war. By now the two daughters in the household were long married, but during the war, their father had wanted me to marry one of the daughters. We then traveled to Germany, first taking a Rhine river cruise and then visiting the charming wine town of Rüdeshime am Rhein. In Luxembourg, we were entertained by an official there and given a banquet, where we enjoyed a nice view of the capital city, which is set dramatically on hills and in two gorges. Luxembourg survived WWII without too much damage. We then went to a place that held many memories for me: the battlefields of the "Battle of the Bulge," which still showed the ravages of the war. The locals were able to locate for our group the very spot in Bastogne, Belgium, where I had set up our unit's aid station in a railway station in late December 1944. It looked over the battlefield.

In 2003, John revisiting the railway station in Bastogne where he had set up an aid station during the Battle of the Bulge in December 1944.

From Bastogne, our group crossed the Rhine into Germany. The last time I was there, in January of 1945, what we crossed was a pontoon bridge. Interestingly, our tour guide, who had spent a major part of his youth in Berchtesgaden, Germany, knew this area very well. He took us to a cave that had, at one point, been filled with thousands of valuable items (paintings, sculptures, etc.) stolen from the Jews and meticulously catalogued by the Germans. The cave was very dry, so it was a good place to store delicate works of art. The Allied forces discovered the trove of treasures as they liberated the region.

We then continued on to the Berghof, Hitler's home at the top of a mountain in the Obersalzberg of the Bavarian Alps in Germany. The compound was like a castle, fortified all around, as was the road leading up to the Berghof. The residence was furnished in a very German style. I enjoyed touring the building and picturing Hitler hiding out there during the war.

Our last stop was a delightful music festival in Salzburg, Austria, birthplace of Mozart. Our charming guide, who was part German and part French, had a lovely singing voice. In the evenings, he sang German and French songs to us. We would go to dinner, and he would sing and play the guitar, and after returning to our hotels, the rest of the group would party, drinking all the local libations. Our last night with the group was a pleasant wrap-up to a trip that was filled with many poignant moments. Gwen and I kept in touch with many of the people we met on that memorable trip. It was good for me to see that there had been parts of Europe that were really not engaged in the war, and at the same time, the tour painted a picture for us of what was happening in the rest of Germany while the Nazis were fighting in the rest of Europe. It was heartwarming to see places that hadn't been bombed and had retained their Old World charm and history. We appreciated having all of the police protecting us on the trip. And what better way to wrap up our highlights of this WWII trip than a stopover on our way home to San Francisco for a few days in Paris, a city that is also a part of my story as a combat medic. I first discovered the many joys of Paris when I was able to go there on leave from the fighting after the city had been liberated by the Allies.

Wars are a terrible way to solve international problems, but what do nations do when faced with a situation like this, where another country was killing millions of Jews, gypsies, and many other groups that were targeted by a despotic madman? This trip, though, showed me that healing can happen. In the end, this tour was extremely cathartic for me.

CHAPTER FIFTEEN

Washington, DC—French Legion of Honor Medal
• 2007

The publication of the 35th Infantry Division in which I served, the *Santa Fe Express Divisionnaire*, comes to me regularly. Sometime in 2005, it posted a notice that combat veterans of World War II would be eligible for the French Legion of Honor, France's highest order of merit. If one was interested, he or she should send some basic information to the local French consulate for consideration. I sent my information in. It was acknowledged, but I heard nothing else. Obviously, there was no guarantee that there would be a French Legion of Honor medal in my future.

In the late afternoon of Friday, October 26, 2007, I got a phone call from the French consulate in San Francisco. The man calling asked if it would be possible for me to come by the consulate that afternoon or evening, as the new French consul general would like to speak with me. He would be leaving for Paris that evening. If it were not possible to meet that day, they would try to arrange something the following week. However, it was clearly implied that the visit on the 26th would be desirable. I said that I lived close by the consulate and asked if it would it be convenient if I were to come right over. The distance was only six or seven blocks from where I live. He was pleased with that. I put on a decent blazer and took off.

The consulate is on the fourth floor of a nice office building on Bush Street. I rang the bell and was greeted by a young man immediately. There was a reception area, from which I was taken to a large area with a number of desks. I was introduced to various members of the staff and was surprised to see these many workers there that late in the day. Finally, the deputy consul general, Patrice Servantie, introduced me to the new consul general, Pierre-François Mourier. He met me graciously and took me and Patrice into his office, a fairly large space with elegant leather furnishing. I was shown to a sofa facing a large desk, behind which sat Pierre. He was a medium-sized, well-dressed man who spoke English well with a pleasant French accent.

After some brief small talk, Pierre asked if it would be possible for me to go to Washington, DC, the week of December 5th. I replied yes, I thought it would be possible. He then said that the newly elected president of France, Nicolas Sarkozy, was to be in Washington briefly, and he would like to award me the French Legion of Honor. That was a mind-blowing surprise. After I pulled myself together, I said that this was very short notice to get air reservations. He said that would be no problem. They would take care of that. Then I said that I could not go to such an important occasion without my wife. He said they would gladly provide for her. I mentioned the fact that hotel reservations might be difficult. He said that they would take care of that. He also stated that they would get us to the airport and see that we got to the hotel in DC. It all sounded wonderful.

There was some brief talk about the event. Essentially, there were to be seven veterans of World War II chosen from around the country. I was to represent the Western US. He said that they were particularly impressed with the fact that someone with my background—being a student and in training as an OB-GYN intern—could adapt to combat conditions and be recognized for doing an excellent job. I asked how I should dress for the occasion. I said I could still fit into my uniform if they would like that. He thought the uniform would be excellent for the presentation of the medal, but on the following day we were to go to Congress to hear Mr. Sarkozy speak, and that would be followed by a luncheon. For those two events, I would need to wear the medal on a business suit.

I floated home. Naturally, Gwen and I were very excited. We quickly notified our children. The next day, my daughter, Jan, began making plans to join us. I checked with the consulate, and they said they would be able to reserve a room for her in our hotel, and they also could get her on the same plane. They also said that we would have to pay for her, which we were happy to do.

My younger son Jim and his wife, Sheryl, live in Chico. On hearing the news, they immediately made plans to join us. They made their own hotel reservations, since they had a relationship with Hyatt. My older son, John, was out of town at a medical meeting, but when he returned, he also decided to join us. But by this time he had great difficulty getting a plane reservation, but he finally got on a "red eye," arriving late on the evening of November 4th. He couldn't find a hotel room, but the staff at the hotel where we were staying suggested he share a room with our daughter. They could put in a rollaway.

We were to leave on the morning of the 5th of November. That morning we were packed with carry-on luggage; Jan, who lives only a short distance away, joined us. Pierre appeared right on time with a French government van and driver; he would be accompanying us. We were traveling on United Airlines. Gwen and I were Frequent Fliers. We had checked on our seats and found that we were sitting behind each other. I called repeatedly to get the seats improved. Finally, I got a supervisor, who said she would put in a request. Jan had an aisle seat in the middle of the economy section. Pierre had a terrible seat far back in economy. (The French instructions to consulates are that their staffers must travel economy. I later told Pierre that he should get an agent who could get him much better economy seats in the future.) At the gate, just before boarding, Gwen and I were paged, and we were presented with seats far back in business class, which was wonderful for us.

The trip was uneventful. Upon our arrival in DC, Pierre called the man who was to meet us on his cell phone. The man had been at the luggage collecting point, but we, of course, had carry-on. The man, a French major, drove us to our hotel, The Park Hyatt. Though the woman at reception gave us a lot of trouble, mainly because of her inexperience, we were finally taken to our rooms. Gwen and I had a pleasant, small suite. Much to our joy, Jan had a double room with two beds, which would work well when my son, John, arrived much later.

Gwen and I went to the hotel bar for a snack. While sitting there, a gentleman came over and asked if we were there for the medal, and we said we were. He introduced himself as another recipient. He was an American Indian named Charles Shay, traveling with his chief and former chief. He is a remarkable man. He was in the first wave in the invasion of North Africa, in the first wave in the invasion of Sicily, and in the first wave in the invasion of Normandy. All of his wartime service was with the 1st Infantry Division. Later on he served in the Korean War. He was modest about all of this. It was a good introduction to the type of people who were to get the medal on the following day.

We decided to spend the next morning doing nothing special. The big event was to occur in the afternoon of the 5th of November. At breakfast and in various areas, we had a chance to meet the other recipients. Senator Daniel Inouye was the only one not staying at our hotel, since he had his own residence in DC. James Hill was with the 29th Division, which was in the first wave at Omaha Beach. Henry Langrehr was a parachutist who landed behind the German lines with the 82nd Airborne the day before D-Day. He was wounded, captured, hospitalized, put to work in a coal mine, and escaped with a buddy, who was killed. He was wounded two more times before the end of the war. George Thompson had a remarkable record as a mortar man. Bernie Rader, a small man from New York, had memorized the eye chart in order to get into the service. He was wounded, captured, and exchanged, and returned to fight on. These were the sort of people who made me feel doubly honored to be included.

We were to be at the residence of the French ambassador at 3:30 p.m. I put on my World War II uniform right before a small fleet of vans came to pick us up way in advance of the event. Jan and John traveled with Gwen and me, and Jim and his wife were to meet us at the residence. By chance, we all arrived at the same time.

The residence is a splendid building built in 1905 and bought by France in 1936. It sits on five acres of lush gardens. We all went through security quickly. They were well-prepared. There were gracious people everywhere who introduced themselves and took us to the large room where the presentation was to take place. The medal recipients were seated in reserved seats in the first row of chairs. Other chairs were placed behind for family and close friends. The large space gradually filled with men in military uniforms of France and the US. There were more photographers than I have ever seen in such a relatively small area. While we were waiting for French President Sarkozy to arrive, two of us were interviewed at length. Jim and Sheryl came to watch.

President Sarkozy was in Washington for only twenty-six hours and had an extremely busy schedule, so it was not surprising that he was late by twenty minutes or so. He came in a relaxed manner and was introduced by a French officer. He spoke in French even though he speaks good English. He had an excellent translator who timed her translations perfectly. Essentially, he expressed the gratitude of France for what we and the people with whom we fought did for France in liberating it from the Germans. He then gave a brief biography of each of us recipients. He displayed a sense of humor when he said that Charles Shay, the American Indian, had an ancestor in the seventeenth century who was a French trapper, which meant that Shay had deeper roots to France than Sarkozy did.

John being awarded the French Legion of Honor medal by French President Nicolas Sarkozy.

He then went down the line of us. He pinned a medal on our lapels, kissed us on each cheek, and gave us an embrace. When he did that with me, I said, "Merci." He quickly responded, "Thank you, JOHN, you are a hero." I was impressed that he had learned my name.

He then had his picture taken with all of us and quietly left. The ceremony was followed by a splendid reception held in the dining room, which had beautiful pale green boiserie (wood paneling). The food and drink were sumptuous. There was foie gras, plus elegant French champagne and all kinds of other tidbits and wine. I was pleased to see that my children made themselves at home and talked with various guests, especially the French, many of whom were veterans of World War II. I had the opportunity to talk with the commanding general of the 10th Mountain Division, in which I had served in the United States before being transferred to the 35th for the invasion of Normandy. The general looked like a college student to me, but his division is one of the most respected. I told him how what I had learned in the 10th Mountain helped me and those I cared for survive in the Ardennes in the Battle of the Bulge. We left the residence on schedule.

    Gwen and I had arranged dinner that evening at a restaurant where we had celebrated our fiftieth wedding anniversary in 1996. We all arrived at the same time and, after a bit of negotiation, we were gathered in the same area, so we could celebrate our big sixty-first anniversary. Obviously, everyone had a lot to talk about. On the following day, Gwen and I were invited to hear Sarkozy address the US Congress. Tickets were limited. Sheryl had been working to get tickets for her, Jim, John, and Jan. Frankly, we didn't think she would be able to do it.

    On the following morning, Gwen and I were picked up. We hoped to see our children later or maybe in San Francisco. All of the medal honorees were wearing their medals as instructed. We were taken to an elegant reception room in the Capitol building. Much to our pleasant surprise, we saw Sheryl, Jim, John, and Jan as we marched past. Somehow or other Sheryl had obtained tickets for all of them, even though the gallery was sold out. In the reception room, Speaker of the House Nancy Pelosi came by to congratulate all of us and to have her picture taken with the group, but before she did that she greeted Gwen and me, her constituents, and had her picture taken with just us. We then went to take our seats in the diplomatic gallery. Gwen and I were assigned to the first row, and much to our surprise and joy, all of our children were seated right behind us. Medal winners were supposed to get one seat, but somehow our daughter-in-law, Sheryl, had swung the deal.

John at the residence of the French ambassador on the day of the award ceremony.

The congressional floor, the balcony, and the diplomatic areas were all full. Both houses of Congress and the members of the Supreme Court were there. President

Sarkozy was introduced by Pelosi, who was chair of the event. Sarkozy spoke beautifully in French. We all had earphones with instant translation. He got repeated applause and several standing ovations. It had been a long time since a French president had come to the US and a long time since there was something to cheer about. He stressed the French debt to the US, particularly in World War II. He also made a major point of how we should work together to improve the environment and promote world peace.

After the congressional session, the medal recipients and one guest each were invited to a special luncheon at the French embassy. The embassy is a working building, interesting but quite modern. We were all seated at assigned seats. Present in addition to the medal winners and their guests were French veterans, some military men, and various members of the diplomatic staff.

The luncheon was pleasant. One of the French guests, an older man, told Gwen that he enjoyed meeting and talking with Jan on the previous day. At the end of the meal, I thought that I should say something especially because President Sarkozy had called me the "dean" of the group. I made a short speech of thanks for the gracious way we had been treated.

We arrived back home in San Francisco tired but still excited. We were met at the San Francisco airport by a driver who took Gwen and me home, then Jan, then Pierre. As tired as we were, we did not sleep too well. Our minds were busy reliving those splendid few days.

> **From Gwen's travel diary**: *[After flying home to San Francisco,] we were exhausted, but it was an incredible experience. The whole time we were in Washington it felt like we were in Paris. Back home we received a phone call from our cousin in France who told us that he had seen the whole*

ceremony in Congress that day on TV and saw us sitting in the front row of the gallery.

Word got around the UCSF medical center and elsewhere, and I began to get congratulatory letters and phone calls shortly after our trip to DC, but there was no significant newspaper mention of Sarkozy's visit.

*John wearing his old WWII dress uniform; a close-up of his medal (*San Francisco Chronicle, *December 17, 2007; photos by Liz Hafalia).*

However, in early December, I got a call from John Koopman, a reporter for the *San Francisco Chronicle*. He wanted to interview me. We set up a date, and he came to our apartment. He is a big, affable man and a former Marine, though I think once a Marine always a Marine. We had a pleasant, long session. He had been embedded with the 1st Marine Division in the invasion of Iraq. These things being so, he seemed to understand what it is that a combat medic does. He asked if he could send a photographer. Of course, I had no objection. She came a couple of days later and must have taken a hundred shots of me in the uniform I wore during WWII. In a few days, Koopman called to say that his editor liked the story. So I thought there would be a piece about me in some Sunday supplement. Early on the morning of December 17th, I got a call from my son, John, and his wife, Louise, that I was on the front page of the *Chronicle*. It was a lengthy article that included a picture of me and could not have been more complimentary.

Now the phone calls and mail really poured in: various people at the medical center, including Doctor Bishop, the chancellor; Senator Dianne Feinstein, the consul general of Belgium, who presented me with a signed picture of her king and queen; and so many more. The San Francisco Gynecological Society asked to honor me. The internet contained much more, including many photos surrounding the event. At this point in my life, I was not prepared for such attention, but it was wonderful.

Nonetheless, in sum, nothing has been more rewarding in my life than the nearly seventy-five years of wedded bliss with my loyal traveling companion, Gwen. We married a short time after we met because we thought we would get along together. Our long, happy life as husband and wife proved that and then some. The travels we shared together helped make our marriage even more perfect. You might say this book chronicling our travels is one long love letter to her. I hope you've enjoyed it.

On the road again!

ABOUT THE AUTHOR

John A. Kerner, MD

John A. Kerner, MD, has been one of the most esteemed leaders of San Francisco and California's medical community and helped immeasurably to bring forward-thinking practices to the state. In addition to his OB-GYN practice, he served as Mount Zion Medical Center Chief of Staff and UCSF Clinical Professor. He was one of just seven US WWII veterans awarded the French Legion of Honor by French president Nicolas Sarkozy in Washington, DC, in 2007. Dr. Kerner is also the author of *Combat Medic, World War II* (2012), *A Combat Medic Comes Home* (2012), and *San Francisco Heroes I Have Known* (2015). All are published by iBooks; *Combat Medic* is now available in a hardcover edition.